LIVING WITH THE PAST

LIVING WITH THE PAST

Henry Sandon

Hodder & Stoughton
LONDON SYDNEY AUCKLAND

First published in Great Britain in 1997

1 3 5 7 9 10 8 6 4 2

British Library Cataloguing in Publication Data
A record for this book is available from the British Library

ISBN 0 340 69426 2

Typeset by Avon Dataset Ltd, Bidford-on-Avon, Warks

Printed and bound in Great Britain by
Mackays of Chatham PLC, Chatham, Kent

Hodder and Stoughton Ltd
A Division of Hodder Headline PLC
338 Euston Road
London NW1 3BH

Contents

My name is Henry Sandon and I'm a potaholic.

I'm also founder president of Potaholics Anonymous, a society for people like me who can't keep their hands off pots. In fact they have to have a new piece of pottery or porcelain each day in order to satisfy their craving. But it was not always thus. . . .

1

Family Pictures

I was born in Charing Cross Hospital, well within the sound of Bow Bells, so am technically a Cockney, and very proud of that. My birthplace is now no longer in Charing Cross – the hospital has removed to West London – and it is upsetting to find that my first home has also gone west. Newport Buildings, where I lived for my first few years, was a tenement lying between lower Charing Cross Road and Newport Street, and is now covered over by Chinatown.

When people ask me when I was born I usually answer, 'The same day as Queen Elizabeth the Queen Mother'. That usually causes a few raised eyebrows until I hasten to say, 'Not the same year, of course!', for she is as old as the century; but it is wonderful to have the full national anthem played on the radio each 4th August. If you really need to know the year, then it was 1928, an interesting time to be brought up in Soho, which was a very cosmopolitan area, full of fascinating people and specialist businesses, with no trace of the sleaze that developed later. In fact the streets were my playground and I felt as safe as houses. The photograph of me playing the violin with dog Bob in front of Newport Buildings will give you an idea of what things were like.

My family were deeply involved in music and the arts. I was an only child but my mother was one of twelve children – the seventh daughter of a seventh daughter, she told me. That was supposed to produce mystical powers, but I never saw any trace of those in her. Her father, George Mellish (I was given the middle name George after him), was a professional violinist and made and sold violins and music. Grandpa and Grandma, whose maiden name was Cave, produced a succession of daughters every two years – Alice, Rosie, Dora, Florence and Winnie – and must have despaired of producing a son until Lionel appeared in 1892. Then it was a varied sequence: a daughter who died soon after birth, then Reg, Clara (my mother), Ruby, Leslie and Vera, the baby of the family, who is still alive. The family were especially proud of their descent from Colonel Henry Mellish, who is credited with the composition of the beautiful tune to 'Drink to me only with thine eyes', though most publications insist that it is a folk song. He was a Regency rake who lost all his money in gambling.

Most of the family were musical, playing instruments or singing, and gatherings at the family home in Harlesden always involved concerts with the family orchestra or singsongs round the piano. When I was taken there I was always expected to sing the latest music-hall song that I had heard, or a song taught to me at school, and my earliest sad memories were of singing to Grandma when she was ill in bed. Her death hit Grandpa very hard. They were a devoted couple and two days after she died he went out for a walk, returned home and died peacefully, from a broken heart, my mother said. They were buried together in Kensal Green cemetery.

My oldest aunt, Alice, was always known as Doll or Dolly. She was a professional pianist and accompanied silent films with composed or improvised music, fitting it to the mood of the scene up on the screen. I loved the galloping music as the posse of cowboys tore off after the baddies, but thought less of the love scenes which she usually accompanied by Elgar's 'Salut d'Amore'. For better-class cinemas she would join Grandpa's band to play specially composed scores, which had to be very carefully timed with the scene. Luckily I had free admission to all the palaces of joy and, being born into the last few years of the silent cinema, will never forget the romance of it all. Dolly's best appointment was as the organist of the Stoll Opera House in Leicester Square, which interspersed films with stage turns; it later became the great Odeon cinema.

Being the oldest, Dolly took over the guiding reins of the family after the death of my grandparents. On occasions I was sent to stay with her for a weekend or a few days and I was always a bit scared of doing something wrong as she was a prim and proper Victorian lady. Listening to the wireless, if the announcer

5

coughed she would say, 'Rude man!' in a very angry voice – I can hear her now – and I gathered that she did not have a great regard for men; perhaps that was through having mainly sisters to look after. I remember being sent to look under her bed before I turned in, to see if there was a man lurking there. When I told my mother this she said, 'Dolly won't be lucky to find one!' But she did, years after a long musical career in which she played for the family concert party on the seaside sands and running her own orchestra, the Catherine Startup's Ladies Orchestra (actually a trio) at Trump's Café in Sidmouth. She finally married, quite late in life, a charming man who had courted her for years, only for the marriage to founder at the reception. They never saw each other again, though he used to send her a parcel of socks and pants each week, which she would dutifully wash, iron and post back.

There were no other aunts or uncles quite as eccentric as Dolly. I was closest to Ruby and Leslie, who were my godparents, and would spend holidays with Rosie at Burnham and Dora at Brightlingsea, ensuring a week or so at the sea, or with Lionel in Birmingham. All my aunts and uncles bar one are dead; Vera is the remaining one and still plays the piano most beautifully. One of her favourite tasks was playing for ballet classes and during the second world war, as a member of ENSA (often called by the troops 'Every Night Something Awful') she was one of the many small groups who entertained the troops or workers in munition factories. One day Vera turned up in High Wycombe, where I was at school, and we had lunch in a restaurant and spent the afternoon in a cinema watching *Dangerous Moonlight* with Anton Walbrook. I can never hear the Warsaw Concerto without thinking of that lovely day.

I hope the other aunts and uncles would not mind my calling Florence Vivienne the most famous of them. Starting her life as a singer, with her first concert at the Wigmore Hall, she quickly became seduced by the camera lens, married an art teacher, Ernest Entwhistle, and chose as her professional name Vivienne. They had a romantic studio in St John's Wood with a wonderful basement in which, as a special treat, I was allowed to play with my cousins and their friends. She started her photographic work there, then realised that a West End base was necessary to break into the high-class world of society studio photography. After a happy period in a flat in Sackville Street, just off Piccadilly, they took over a war-torn building in Hamilton Mews, at the bottom of Park Lane.

In her first book, *They Came to my Studio*, published by Hall Publications in 1956, she reminisces about the many famous people who sat for her there. These included all our Prime Ministers from Sir Winston Churchill to Edward Heath (their photographs are in a place of honour on the long staircase of No. 10 Downing Street) and many great political figures. There were also people from the world of the arts,

especially the stage, film and ballet, and all her sub-
jects praised her ability to put them at their ease and
to produce some of the most telling subjects of our
time. Just some of the names of these sitters read
like a roll-call of the famous actors of a golden age:
Dame Sybil Thorndike, Sir Laurence Olivier, Vivienne
Leigh, Sir John Gielgud, Dame Peggy Ashcroft, Sir
Cedric Hardwicke, Robert Morley, Dame Flora
Robson, Emlyn Williams, John Clements, Sir Kenneth
More, Dame Wendy Hiller, Sir Peter Ustinov, the two
Hermiones – Baddeley and Gingold – Dorothy Tutin,
Renée Asherson, Sir John Mills and Rossano Brazzi.
The list just goes on and on. The world of ballet,
radio, the arts and music included Dame Alicia
Markova, Dame Margot Fonteyn, Sir Anton Dolin,
Dame Ninette de Valois, Moira Shearer, Sir Robin
Day, John Snagge, Malcolm Muggeridge, Pietro
Annigoni, Kathleen Ferrier, Adèle Leigh, Louis
Kentner, Eileen Joyce and Anne Ziegler and Webster
Booth.

Many photographs of the Churchill family were
taken, both at the studio where the famous one of Sir
Winston sitting on a chair with a bulldog expression
on his face was taken (later used on a fine Spode vase)
and at his home – Chartwell. Some of these were
taken by one of Vivienne and Ernest's two sons,
Anthony Roger Entwhistle, who was the Crown
photographer with Wingate's troops in the Burma
campaign. He used his two Christian names when he
made his own studio photographs, and then changed

his name by deed poll to Beauchamp. Anthony Beauchamp, or Tony as I knew him, became very friendly with Sir Winston's actress daughter Sarah, and I have a fun photograph of the wedding party taken by Tony himself, a delayed action shot allowing him to be in the photograph. When Tony asked the great man for his daughter's hand he told me that he was quaking at the knees but permission was gladly given. Tony thought it was the quality of the photographs that swung it, but regrettably the marriage did not last long. Tony's brother Clive went into business and became a partner with the firm of surgical boot makers Gilbert and Mellish, founded by Alex Gilbert, who married my grandparents' second daughter Rosie, and Lionel Mellish, their oldest son. This fine business is still going strong in Selly Oak, Birmingham. Alex and Rosie were leading lights in pierrot concert parties, very popular on the sands and piers of English seaside resorts in the 1920s and 30s. One group was called 'The Scarleteers' – you can imagine the colour of their costumes. Another was 'The Military Mummers' and Dolly was the pianist. When needed, other members of the family would be pressed in to perform, especially those who had fine voices or played instruments, and Alex did a magic act called 'Firelight Dreams'.

It was into this maternal side of the family that I threw myself with great gusto as there were always huge numbers of aunts, uncles and cousins, now sadly much depleted. You'll be asking by now, 'But what about your father?' He had come over from Italy after the first world war to become a naturalised British citizen working as a restaurant waiter and manager in such famous restaurants as the Ritz Hotel and Oddenino's. A chance meeting with my mother Clara when he went into the attractive Fancy Dress Photographic Studios in Oxford Street to have his photograph taken led to them instantly falling in love. My mother not only took photographs but coloured them in with watercolours; Vivienne, Ruby and Vera would be pressed into service when orders came in thick and fast. You could dress up in a fancy dress costume to have your photograph taken and Vera remembers a full-sized aeroplane in the window of the Oxford Street shop. Customers could dress up like Amy Morrison and be photographed about to take off on a round-the-world flight, although the aeroplane would not have got very far as it was purely a mock-up.

After marriage, my parents ran a restaurant in Brewer Street in Soho, not very far from Newport Buildings, and I spent a lot of my early years there. The restaurant (I suppose you would call it a café nowadays) was called the British Restaurant and catered largely for the Berwick Street market stall holders nearby. There they would be regaled with good, solid English dishes and low, low prices. My parents would pop in a strangely named dish, such as 'Princess Marina's wedding cake' to celebrate a royal wedding. They were still living in Newport

Buildings and it was there that I was brought up into the strange world that my father was to inhabit until the war – training dogs for the cinema. His first dog, named Bob because he cost five bob (five shillings, or twenty-five pence nowadays) in Club Row market in the East End on a Sunday morning, was a lovely, kind dog with the sweetest temper you could imagine. He would let me do anything I liked with him, allowing me to dress him up and ride on him, and it was this easy-going nature of this scruffy but appealingly happy dog that led my father to teach him tricks. Dad taught him over fifty tricks, such as playing dead when shot with a blank, rescuing a child, or anything you wanted, and Mother's photographs were sent to film studios who began to think that Bob could be the British rival to Rin Tin Tin, the American canine film star.

Bookings poured in and Dad was kept busy travelling to the large number of British film studios that sprang up on the outskirts of London to produce quickly made films to fulfil the quota system. This ensured that if an American film went on general release in this country then there had to be a British 'B' movie to balance it on the same show. Masses of films poured out of these studios, many using Bob. The titles must have given the audience a good idea of the plot of Bob's films – four silent epics, *Cocktails* with Monty Banks (later to marry Gracie Fields), *Down Channel*, a New Era movie, *The Wickham Mystery* with the beautiful Eve Gray (a G. B. Samuelson production), and the film in which Bob was the eponymous hero and stray, *Scrags, the Tale of a Dog*. I think the title was meant to be a pun and the story is of a child who was kidnapped (the child was me) and Scrags sets off round London to find him and drag him back to his parents. As my father was the tramp owner of the dog in the film, you can imagine the joyful reunion. The studio seemed to be happy with the reception of this three-reel epic (ten minutes a reel, so thirty minutes of film). They booked the dog for more films when the talkies arrived: *Poor Old Bill, Compromising Daphne, My Wife's Family* and *The Outsider*, all by BIP Studios; *Contraband Love* by B and D and *Paper Chase* by United Artists (a prestigious booking this) and of course *The Cockney Kid*, a take-off of the American film *The Kid*, in which I played the Jackie Coogan part.

But it was becoming evident that Bob was not cut out for talkies, as he did his best tricks when words of command were given by my father – not much use when the film was with sound. So back to Club Row went my father, mother and I to find another dog. Actually it was not my father who found Bob number two – it was Bob who found Dad. This battered, poorly treated cross between a Welsh collie and fifty-six other varieties stopped my father in his tracks with such an appealingly hopeful look that he nearly fell for him straightaway. He walked on hoping to find a better looking dog, but wherever he went he would turn and see the dog's eyes following him.

Dad said, 'That's the one,' and another five bob changed hands. Bob the second proved to be an avid pupil, once he had had a bath and a lot of love, but never quite became the easy-going dog that his predecessor had been. Film studios had to take out special insurance in case Bob savaged their leading lady, and I remember his last film, *The Thief of Baghdad*, when a huge negro has to pick up Bob and after Conrad Veidt snarls at Bob (who has been changed from Sabu, playing Abu the thief) the dog fights back until he is tossed into the sea (a dummy was used for that, of course). But when the negro tried to put Bob down, the dog turned on him with such ferocity that the poor man had to be taken to hospital.

So life with Bob was always fraught with worry, but teach him a trick once and it was there for ever. Dad would send him off with a penny in his mouth to buy a particular paper and I swear that dog could read because he always came back with the right one. The film studios would ring up and ask if Bob could come and do such and such a scene at Pinewood, Elstree or Shepperton; my father would teach him the trick and the dog would do it first take the next day.

I suppose the most embarrassing day of my young life was when the studios rang to ask if the dog would do a scene next morning with Claude Hulbert, the silly-ass brother of Jack Hulbert. The story line is that Claude is hanging onto a lamppost, drunk; the dog wanders by, lifts his leg and does what dogs do on lampposts, but in this case all over Claude. My father said, 'We've trained him *not* to do things like that,' but they asked him to have a shot. He hit on the idea of taking Bob around Soho that night and I was given a cloth. Wherever Bob wanted to lift his leg, my father reasoned that there must be a very good smell, and I had to dash in with the cloth and wipe it up before Bob covered it. I remember hoping that none of my school friends would see me during the half-hour walk, and wondering all the time at the wonderful skill of a dog being able to squeeze out a few drops at a time.

The limousine pulled up outside Newport Buildings early next morning and all the kids in the neighbourhood poured out to see Dad and me with Bob carrying his own attaché case containing the impregnated cloth, climbing into the back of the car. It was an early morning shot and Dad wiped the cloth over the artificial lamppost. Claude Hulbert came on the set, told to be drunk (he made a very good drunk), and hung on the lamppost but wasn't told what was going to happen. The clapper boy marked the shot, my father released Bob, who wandered up to the post, sniffed at it with joy beaming all over his face. He lifted his leg and all over Claude Hulbert went the results, to the actor's obviously real horror. The producer shouted 'Cut and print!' and all the studio hands burst into spontaneous applause. But you will never see that scene if you are lucky to see the film *Big Business*, as the censor thought it too disgusting to be shown, and cut it out.

Bob appeared in about twenty films, for such companies as G.B., Fox, Butchers and Warner Brothers. Both Dad and I had bit or walking on parts in some of these and the dog appeared with some of the most celebrated film stars of the day, such as the Soho-born Jessie Matthews in *Head over Heels*, Skeets Gallagher in *Mr Satan*, ex-heavyweight boxer Jack Doyle in *McClusky the Sea Rover*, Leslie Fuller in *Big Hearted Bill*, Cicely Courtneidge in *Everybody Dance* and Will Hay in *Where There's a Will*.

But his greatest film was to be his last. We had left Newport Buildings and the Berwick Street café to take a larger café in Camden Town. I didn't like moving from Soho, where I had so many friends and liked St Anne's school. Almost every race under the sun was there and I learned to get on with all races and creeds. Even the smells of Soho were something special, from the freshly baked bread at Rosen's shop to the terrible smell of tar being melted in machines to lay on the wood blocks of the street. When the men turned up to do this I was told to hurry out and sniff the tar as it would do me good. My father bought me what he was told was a canary in Club Row but the thing wouldn't sing in its cage, only chirp. Of course it turned out to be a duckling and used to follow me while I pedalled round Soho in my pedal car – I think it was supposed to be Malcolm Macdonald's 'Bluebird' car. Regrettably the poor little creature met his end under the wheels of my car.

The most interesting character in Soho in those days ran the newspaper shop on the corner of Newport Court – Johnny Fisher, or Johnny Schofield as he called himself in films, where he did an enormous number of small character parts, having the sort of face that fitted into any sort of scene you could think of. I did a lot of publicity photographs mainly for Fox Photos, such as in the arms of the giant Italian world heavyweight boxer, Primo Carnera, punching him on the nose.

Camden Town was a very different area. I hated the school there and made up any excuse to my mother to prevent me from going. The worst thing was the smell of the Black Cat cigarette factory just down the road and I'm sure that put me off cigarettes for life. But there were some compensations – I could get any number of fag cards and swap them to build up sets of Howlers or Cricketers or my favourite, which was Henry, a funny little lad with a wisp of hair who was always thinking up schemes to earn money. As the manufacturing company's name was Kensitas, my nickname at school was 'Kensitas', which drove me mad but I still have my two complete sets of Henry. Another interesting thing was wrestling at the local baths and Mother would get into a real tizzy, screaming out 'Kill him!' or 'Tear his arm off!', although she was a very gentle person away from the ring. Dad's interest was playing a strange game of bar billiards on a small table in the café. He became quite a genius at this, playing a brilliant game against all comers, and used to play double or quits with the milkman and bread man. If the challenger lost, my father paid nothing; if Dad lost he paid double. Dad hardly ever lost – he hadn't been brought up on the crane-grab machines in Soho fun-fairs for nothing – and after a few months he had few challengers. Another thing that fascinated him was going to the early meetings of Sir Oswald Mosley's fascist Blackshirts and he would take me along some-times. I must say, it was mesmerising to listen to Mosley. Such intensity is seldom heard nowadays. But after a riot and fight with the police my mother stopped us from going, so after that our most exciting event was going to Hyde Park Corner to listen to the speakers and heckle them.

We moved again in 1935 to Peckham where in Queen's Road Dad had his last shop: a newspaper, tobacconist's and soft drinks shop. I had my first bicycle and it was thrilling to cycle round the streets of Peckham, really very safe as there was not a lot of traffic. We had trade boards outside the shop for music halls, theatres and cinemas and were given free tickets, provided we went on a Monday, the smallest house of the week. But what a joy it was to see the great names of British music hall – Wee Georgie Wood, Wilson, Keppel and Betty with their sand dance, George Robey (the Prime Minister of Mirth), Old Mother Riley, Elsie and Doris Waters, the great George Formby and the Cheeky Chappie himself –

Max Miller. Other places to which I loved to go were the Holborn Empire and the Metropolitan, Edgware Road, both sadly no more. To watch *Sweeney Todd* with Todd Slaughter as the Demon Barber of Fleet Street, ready to slit your throat ('You have a loverly throat for the razor!') before pulling the lever which sent the unsuspecting customer plunging down to the basement where Mrs Lovatt was ready to turn him into succulent meat pies, was joy beyond price.

It was while we were living in Peckham that the Crystal Palace, the showpiece from the Great Exhibition of 1851, burned down. I was hauled out of bed to see the sight – we were just a few miles away – and next day we went to look at the smouldering ruins of what was one of the miracles of the Victorian age.

My health was not good at that time. I'm not really sure what it was but I think it was a run of things like measles and chicken pox, and my eyesight suffered, making it necessary to wear glasses. My fond parents sent me to recuperate with a lovely family who lived in Chalfont St Peter in Buckinghamshire. They had stayed with Jim and Emy Phillips and their children, Joy and Reg, while they were making a film for Denham Studios at the next-door farm at which Jim worked as cowman and pigman. Bob II was playing in a number of scenes and I persuaded my parents to let me stay on when they returned to London. I went to the local village Church of England school, a mile walk each way, and was reminded of the sloping asphalt playground and disgusting toilet block when I was asked to contribute a short article about playground memories for an Amersham school publication. I was thus wonderfully placed to go to see the magical film *The Thief of Baghdad* being shot at Denham Studios.

But with the war looming, I gained a scholarship from Chalfont St Peter school to High Wycombe Royal Grammar School. Mr Williams, the headmaster, announced it to the whole school one memorable morning and I almost fainted with shock.

2

From School to Work

High Wycombe was a small Buckinghamshire market town, famed for making beechwood chairs. It possessed a splendid Royal Grammar School, founded in 1562, which earlier this century moved to new buildings at the top of Amersham Hill, a mile out of the town. My parents had arranged a private evacuation for me, billeting me with the Stevens family, who lived a couple of hundred yards from the school. Private arrangements could often work out better than the fate that befell the many 'little orphans', as they were called, sent to the safety of the countryside from London and other threatened cities and picked willy-nilly as they waited, tired and frightened, on a strange station platform. I have heard many awful stories of the treatment of these little mites since I became a patron of the Evacuees Association and did the presentation of the anniversary reunion service and festival held in the Rhondda for BBC's *Songs of Praise* programme. Not all 'little orphans' were unkindly treated, of course, many finding wonderful homes with their new foster parents, but numbers had a pretty miserable time in a strange environment, leaving their homes with a caseful of belongings, a toy and a gas mask, separated from their parents for the first time in their little lives. You can understand why many returned to their own homes after the first few months of the war, to be re-evacuated after Dunkirk and the build-up to the Blitz.

My parents' action saved me from the Blitz but I used to hear horrific stories of their two years of sheltering each night in Piccadilly tube station, to which they would retreat when the warnings sounded. When they emerged the next morning, they would find out what new bit of London had been hit in the night. They had returned to Soho on the outbreak of war and three of their homes were bombed in turn. Mother said that Hitler was following them around and she was in a flat that was hit by a Saturday morning bomber who flew through Soho, indiscriminately dropping bombs and killing quite a lot of people. Buried under the wreckage, Bob led rescuers to her with his barking but he died shortly afterwards. They only left their beloved London for an odd Sunday, when we would meet at Denham – they would come out on a Green Line bus and I would cycle over and we would have a picnic. For an idyllic couple of hours they were able to forget the war and Dad would pick dandelion leaves, which he loved to eat in salads. Then it was back to the tube for them and High Wycombe for me.

High Wycombe was a fairly peaceful place during the war, as it had few high-profile munitions factories until they started building the lightweight Mosquito fighter there in the many woodworking factories. William Stevens, my foster parent, used to work in one of these and would come home with off-cuts of balsa wood from which Gordon, his younger son, would produce wonderful models of aeroplanes. He tried to get me to do this but I have never been good at such things and I quickly gave it up. The eldest son was Denis, a fine violinist and musician, who was in the sixth form when I went to the RGS. In that 1939/40 year he was in the school play *I Killed the Count* (which made me determined to be in the next play) and gained a scholarship to Oxford; I helped carry some of his cases of books and music to Wycombe station. In the 1950s he became a famous musicologist, specialising in early music, and produced some programmes for the BBC Third Programme in 1956 commemorating the music of the Worcester organist Thomas Tomkins in which I sang, so we met up again after all those years. The *Musical Times* ran a competition for musical clerihews, and I remember one of the winners was about Denis's rather high-brow programmes:

> I'll lay evens
> That Denis Stevens
> Would get the Byrd
> Except on the Third.

Musical readers will not need to be told that Byrd is William Byrd, the great Elizabethan composer. Denis later became a university professor in Canada.

High Wycombe Royal Grammar School then had just over five hundred boys. Now there are over eleven hundred, and the school hall where we performed our plays and had lunch and assembly is filled with computers. When I returned to be speaker and guest of honour at an old boys' reunion I was amazed to see the great new hall and all the other changes. School blocks were built all over the front quadrangle where we used to parade for the Junior Training Corps; more classrooms had replaced the lawns and flower beds which we dug up during the war to grow vegetables; and the 'bogs', our term for the toilet block, had gone. These were great improvements, and it is wonderful to see the annual published exam results which put the RGS in the very top group each year.

I say only five hundred boys but that first year there were many more, as extra boys from Chiswick Grammar School were billeted on us, a complicated arrangement in which we used the school buildings for lessons in the morning while Chiswick used the sports field and then we switched around in the afternoon.

Our headmaster was Mr Edward Tucker, or 'boss' as I was taught by my schoolmates to call him. He was a charming man, although he could cane a miscreant well. He also ran the boarding house with his wife and they would put on a weekly film show for the twenty or thirty boarders and allow me to attend, as I was an evacuee and lived so near. I think he was trying to get me to live at the boarding house, but I didn't quite fancy that. The staff were very varied, most of them being past the age for military service or handicapped or in the forces, or they went in my first year. Some should have retired but were kept on, some were brought back from retirement and there were even women. Imagine our horror when we found that the PT master had changed to a gym mistress – Miss Boddy – and what a girl she was. She used to come in the showers with us to see that we all went under and I understand that after the war she married a member of the staff.

That Christmas holiday in Chalfont introduced me to the wrong side of the law. Rationing was in full swing, especially for meat, and Mr Phillips, who was a genius with pigs, had a sow that he managed to hide from the inspectors who wanted every one recorded so that offspring were only sold to registered butchers and the meat sold on ration. I don't think I can get into trouble after all this time by saying that many houses in the Horn Hill area of Chalfont had a delivery of a package of bits of baby pork by a lad who was learning his lines for the school play while cycling and looking over his shoulder for the police. A big chunk was kept back for the wedding of Joy Phillips.

My part in the play was that of a nurse; the uniform was most becoming and all said that I had fine legs. Mrs Tucker, the headmaster's wife, taught me to walk on high heels and sit like a woman and made a very good job of turning me into a female. But the next year my own voice was going through tumultuous changes, so I couldn't do a school play.

'What's the matter?' I said to the music master, Frederick Bailey, who was also head of the Bucks School of Music.

'Oh, it's sex rearing its ugly head,' he said. 'Try not to sing or speak much during the change.' So I had to get on with school work.

Some teachers I couldn't get on with, some I positively hated. Of maths, not a thing remains, not even the name of the tormentor, who had the habit of going through a complicated theorem turning half around from the board, saying 'Right?' then turning back, rubbing it out and starting something else. But there were some fine ones. Mr Brand was the kindliest of all the teachers. I don't know his age but he seemed a positive ancient deity to us. He must have been well past retirement age but still played cricket for Buckinghamshire. He gave me my first cricket bat, one of his old ones – an ancient Gunn and Moore, bound around the many cracks with thin wires that made a lovely twangy thud that put the fear up the other team. It had to have a name and I called it 'Clickybar' after a bat in one of my favourite stories in the *Hotspur*. The hero would send a hail of hand grenades belting over the Khyber Pass with a blow of Clickybar and I imagined I was doing the same with my shots. I was not a great batsman – Mr Brand said that I decided on the shot before the ball was bowled but having to wear glasses meant that I couldn't wait until it was bowled, otherwise I wouldn't see it at all. But I was better at bowling and became quite good at swinging a ball.

Staff came and went. One year we did Spanish as there was a Spanish teacher available, but it was a disaster. In our class there was a clown named Pinto (there's always one in each class). We would be taught a word – perhaps *el gobernador* – the governor – which the teacher would carefully say: 'El Go berr na dorrr,' or something like that. Round the class he would go, everyone getting it right until he came to master Pinto.

'You say.'

'El Gob on the door,' came the answer.

The poor teacher pulled his hair out in rage. 'Everybody come back on Saturday afternoon!' We had Saturday school to lunchtime but with full class detention nearly every Saturday afternoon we missed a lot of football and cricket for a year.

When the Americans entered the war we had a few teachers from the American air base, up Marlow Hill. My word, they came in like a breath of fresh air – arriving in jeeps, chewing gum and teaching us little. But provided we put on our JTC uniforms they would take us on super trips in the jeeps, either to explore the fascinating Hell Fire Club caves under West Wycombe Hill ('Gee, are they really that old?') or to go to London on two memorable occasions, taking us to the fantastic Rainbow Club in Piccadilly

Circus and then leaving us to our own devices for an hour or two until we met up again for the journey home. My parents were surprised to see their uniformed son at the door. 'You must have Vivienne take you in uniform!' So that was done – I am immortalised in the uniform of Wycombe School JTC.

The Officers' Training Corps (or OTC) changed its name to the Junior Training Corps (JTC) to show that it was not an élitist thing and I had a great time. At first, the uniforms were left-overs from the first world war, with dreadful puttees which took an hour to put on – and Boer war rifles. But in 1943 we received much more up-to-date new uniforms and equipment. With Lee Enfield 303s to actually fire we became a great fighting force, enough to put the fear of God up the local Home Guard or 'Dad's Army'. I learned to crawl along like a snake, hide in a clump of grass suitably camouflaged and jump out on unsuspecting sheep. (In those days there were fields opposite the school where we played soldiers; these fields are now covered with housing, for Wycombe has grown up and become a sizable commuter town.) We did regular fire-watching duties at the school at night, getting half a crown (2/6d – 12½p today) for guarding the place; worked on farms for local farmers, harvesting or hoeing cabbages; grew vegetables for the war effort, organised by the woodwork teacher, who could not teach woodwork or metalwork because of a complete lack of raw materials – 'You can't get the wood, you know,' as the Goons put it later.

Finally, school certificate exams came round – the dreaded exams, sat in the school hall in May 1944. I sat there staring at the incomprehensible exam papers before going out of the door to the bogs, wondering if I dared go out and play fives. The push towards Germany had started and we followed the war on maps we made at school. I even organised a form collection for guns for the Russians and received a letter from Mrs Churchill thanking us. A V1 doodle-bug that had overflown London would come throbbing over, but we had to go on with the exams unless the engine cut out (the sign that it was ready to nose-dive). Then it would be 'Under the desks!', and a few moments later a distant explosion. Well, it wasn't us, so back to the exams. I really think we should have been given special credits for sticking out the war, but no.

When I got the results three months later while staying at Chalfont St Peter, I had not done well; brilliant in English language and literature, passes in the easy ones like art, geography and history, and failures in the other things.

So what was I to do with my life? I had thoughts of writing for the *Bucks Free Press*, but that would have involved me staying in Wycombe, which I didn't particularly want. Our careers master suggested a firm of London insurance brokers who were evacuated to Gerrards Cross. I went to see them and they offered me a job, but that would have involved a five-mile cycle ride each way, and I didn't fancy that. I assumed that army service would arrive in 1946 when I was eighteen and I was happy just to swim with the tide until then. Very close to Mr Phillips' house was Newland Park, the evacuated home of the North British and Mercantile Insurance Company. I thought that if the brokers had offered me a job then an insurance company might do so as well. So I went along and got myself a job, starting right away, in the War Department. That sounds terribly important, rather like a government department, but it merely involved issuing policies against damage by war. The two heads of the department were Reginald Painter and Lawrence Wulcko, who found me a willing worker but wet behind the ears. If they were out of our long prefab office and the phone rang, I would answer and be asked if I would take 10% of a million pounds in so-and-so warehouse for three weeks. I would say 'Delighted!' – jolly good business for the company, I thought, writing it down. When Mr Wulcko came back he went very white, asking if I had checked how much we had on that warehouse. Of course I hadn't – well, I didn't even know how to check it. He made a quick phone call, went still whiter and spent the rest of the afternoon ringing up colleagues to lay off most of it. I think he eventually put out nine of the ten per cent that I had taken on so easily. I learned a lesson from that.

The whole thing became a lot of fun. Newland Park was a lovely Georgian mansion with super grounds approached by a driveway less than a mile from Little

Newlands cottage where the Phillips family lived. (It is now a college campus.) Most of the staff had come out from London Head Office, evacuees all, and after working hard all day they needed entertainment in the evening. There were no sizable towns nearby, the nearest village was Chalfont St Giles and Reginald Painter conducted the local choral society in a fine performance of *Elijah*. The baritone soloist who sang the part of Elijah impressed me by singing the whole work without a note of music in front of him – I thought that was wonderful and determined to do the same one day.

Then the war ended and we were given a couple of days off. I dashed up to London to celebrate with my parents and hurried down to Piccadilly Circus to see the fun. Jubilation was everywhere, people climbing up lampposts, getting drunk, kissing everyone in sight, conga dancing in the streets. On to the Palace, and huge crowds milled down through Trafalgar Square, where there were hundreds in the fountains, on top of the lions and trying to scale Nelson. On we pushed through Admiralty Arch in a solid wave of humanity, getting near the palace to join in the chant of 'We want the King, We want the King!' Time after time the royal family came out on the balcony and waved and waved to huge cheers, cries of 'God save the King' and the singing of *Rule Britannia* and the national anthem. I struggled back to Piccadilly Circus in time to see one of Winston Churchill's appearances on the balcony of the Trocadero Hotel, holding up his fingers in his famous 'V for Victory' sign. The crowds were getting more and more excited, there were signs of sexual activity in every doorway and even the police were turning a blind eye – I think they were at it too. As I was just a slip of a lad and not experienced I contented myself with as many passionate kisses from panting young girls as I could stomach and then took myself back to my parents' flat, there to fall exhausted into bed.

Next day it was back to Newland Park, where plans were afoot for the firm to return to London. Now there was not much need of the War Department, I was transferred to the Fire Department, which issued policies against the risk of fire. The company decided that there was really not much point in keeping the hundreds of old insurance policy ledgers running back to the early nineteenth century that were being stored in the basement of a large house in Campden Hill in West London and they could be destroyed, provided that someone checked through them all to extract any policies that might still be in force. I was given the task, together with old Penfold, who was a kind of cleaner/servant to the Fire Department. His main job seemed to consist of bringing round the morning and afternoon tea and, although that cost nothing, if you wanted a clean cup each time Penfold would charge you a shilling a week. He was sad and miserable if you cleaned your own. Penfold was chosen to go with me, supposedly to help with the job, but as he was a white-haired seventy-year-old I didn't fancy his chances much. Anyway, a week or so up in London with pay sounded fine to me.

It was actually a huge task – thousands of massive and heavy ledgers, like you would see on the sloping desk of a Dickensian office, a thousand thick pages in each, all beautifully hand-written in copperplate in ink. The task involved going through every page, checking the policies that might still be in force and consigning the rest for salvage pulping. Lord knows what fascinating facts were destroyed. In recent years a lot of work has been done by Mrs Vulpi on old fire insurance policies, discovering facts about early English porcelain factories that otherwise would be unknown, and I often feel upset about the destruction of those beautiful volumes. But it is no use crying over spilt milk, and I couldn't have kept them, even if I had wanted to. So we were all ready for the move from Newland Park to 61 Threadneedle Street. It was a grand building that had not been damaged much by the war, lying between the Bank of England and the Post Office.

After you walked in through the imposing front door, the ceiling was a good thirty to thirty-five feet high, supported by a range of marble columns that were the colour of corned beef. Built around these was a huge mahogany counter that filled up two opposite sides of this huge space. At the narrower end was another counter with a large gap on the right hand side that led to an imposing marble staircase that seemed to lead to heaven, with the Board Room at the top on the sixth floor. There was a lift for those that could not manage the stairs. The left side, where I was to work, was the main Fire Department where the proposals arrived for processing. I had to check them, put them in a little folder, mark them for the attention of various departments, if needed, like the Guarantee Department in case any part of the cover should be passed on to other companies, or the Streets Department, in case there were any other insurances at the same address – there must not be too many eggs in one basket. The policies were pre-pared at the back of the ground floor, sent to the typists for typing, returned for checking and then sent to the policy holder. The right hand side of the hall was the accounts and cashier's departments, and in front of me sat the managers in their little glass boxes. They had to be consulted if there was anything especially difficult or to sign a problem letter, and you would be called into the box if you were in any trouble.

On my right hand side lay a little passage that ran from the Policy Department to the street, and if you were brave enough you could slip out and get away into the City. My senior, Harold Rattle, then in his early sixties, used to slip out half a dozen times a day, going to different City churches to play the organs. He would be carpeted and taken into the box many times but always seemed to get away with it, after a bit of a row. I too got fascinated by the City, especially the wonderful Wren churches, or at any rate those that had survived the Blitz. I bought a book about them in one of the many secondhand bookshops and, with my great friend Peter Stafford, used to dash to a different one each lunch time. We would return with heads buzzing at the beauty and incredible treasures inside, such as a Grinling Gibbons carving or a triple-decker pulpit. We would slowly tick them off, the nearest ones first – St Mary Woolnoth, St James Garlickhithe, St Edmund King and Martyr. One day we were on London Bridge looking down at the Thames, when a young woman threw herself into the cold, grey, choppy water to drown herself. She obviously regretted it and started splashing and shouting. Without a second thought Peter flung off his coat and shoes, dived in and brought her safely to the North bank. They were both taken to hospital while I returned to Number 61 to explain what had happened. Peter was presented with a special certificate from the City of London police and an award from the King. I can't swim a stroke.

Harold Rattle fostered my first interests in music and I would go out to his home at Bushey, near Watford, to sing with him. We would get through fifty songs each Saturday – Brahms, Schumann, Schubert, Beethoven. Or we would go into his church in Bushey where he was choirmaster and organist and run through some of the simpler cantatas, such as Stainer's *Crucifixion* or Maunder's *Olivet to Calvary*. On Good Friday 1946 I sang the bass solos in the *Crucifixion* in three different London churches for a half guinea a time and much enjoyed it. That experience remained with me when I later got to know Edgar Day, assistant organist of Worcester Cathedral, who had been a great friend of Sir Edward Elgar and had a fund of stories about the grand old man. Edgar asked Sir Edward once, 'What is your opinion of Stainer's *Crucifixion*?' Sir Edward thought for a moment and then said, 'On reflection, I am much in favour of his crucifixion.'

I was seeking to expand my musical learning. I had introduced Harold Rattle to my Uncle Reg, who also lived at Bushey and was a very good cellist. They struck it off and made wonderful music. Then they were introduced by Auntie Ruby to a fine violinist friend and the new trio would spend their holidays at Ruby's house in Lilliput, near Poole Harbour in Dorset. One Sunday evening I had shown Auntie Ruby some of the joys of the City, which was deserted on a Sunday and looked romantic with willow herb growing all over the bomb sites. We went into St Paul's Cathedral for the evening service, accompanied on a piano in the nave by the assistant organist, Harry Gabb. He made an appeal for men to join the reconstructed Sunday Evening Service Choir and I cheekily applied. I had an audition with Dr Dykes-Bower, the lovely and distinguished organist, and was accepted. After a few weeks' rehearsals the choir was ready to sing each Sunday evening, the professional choir singing on weekdays and weekend mornings and afternoons.

It was a wonderful thrill singing in that incredible

building, with an extraordinary echo that seemed to go on for ever. We men had the great advantage of having the cathedral choristers singing with us and though the music was not too complicated at first, there were hymns and a psalm and an anthem. To help out the alto line, one of the professional vicars choral, Victor Masters, would be paid to come in and I was to get to know him very well in the years to come.

I remember my first Watch Night service on New Year's Eve. A big crowd came for the end-of-year service at 11.30 p.m., led by the men of the Sunday Evening Choir, and I walked from home, through the growing excitement in Trafalgar Square, through quiet Fleet Street and into the cathedral. I helped the head virger (vergers of St Paul's always spell their title with an *i* not an *e*) to put out service papers on the chairs under the huge dome. I thought I could see and hear a shadowy figure on the high altar so the virger and I hurried up the chancel steps to one of the holiest places in the country to find a drunken tramp lying sprawled out and singing. The virger shook him by the shoulder and demanded to know what he was doing.

'I'm looking for God,' slurred the drunk.

'Well, you won't find him here,' said the virger, and we hurried him out of the cathedral, leaving him by Queen Anne's statue.

I applied to join the Alexandra Choir, a sizable choral society conducted by Charles Proctor, a very inspiring conductor, who auditioned and accepted me. He was impressed with my ability to sight-read

music, which had been born of my singing with
Harold Rattle and at St Paul's. He also suggested that,
when I was ready, he would recommend me to a good
teacher, but knowing that I was due to do National
Service in a few months' time, that should not be yet.
We rehearsed weekly in a large hall and were preparing for a concert in the Royal Albert Hall – a part
of Bach's B minor Mass and Delius's *Sea Drift*. I
enjoyed it so much I told Harold Rattle, who joined
the choir as well.

Then came the dreaded letter from His Majesty
requesting that I do my duty and protect him and
country for two years, provided I passed the medical.
I did my best to look pretty ghastly – friends at the
office said 'You'll be all right, you'll fail on flat feet or
eyesight,' so I waddled into the church hall to be
processed by a line of doctors.

'Drop your trousers, turn your head away and
cough!'

A cold hand grabbed my genitals and it was done –
I had passed. The order for joining up arrived unless
strong family or business reasons could be put forward. I pleaded that I was the sole support of my
beloved and aged parents, but that was no good. I
asked the departmental head of NBM if he would
put in a plea that I was indispensable, but he would
not. All he did was to shake my hand, wish me well
and tell me that my place would be awaiting me on
my return.

So, off I went to the Army.

3

Competing in Life

The train took us to Devizes in Wiltshire, then, as now, a delightful market town, but I was given no time to appreciate its beauty. Yapping corporals, like sheep dogs, counted us out of the station and into trucks, in which we bumped the one and a half miles to the camp, all eyeing up those who would be our colleagues for the next six weeks of basic training. We were allocated barrack rooms holding thirty each, with a sergeant and two corporals, and were sent to get kitted up. Clothes and strange items of kit came from all directions onto our outstretched arms and I found that I alone among the platoon knew what most of the things were.

Back in the barrack room, the NCOs directed us to try on everything. Very few bits of clothing fitted.

'Never mind, sort that out in the morning. Now, to the cookhouse for supper. Remember to take your irons' – cutlery and mug – 'and make sure you bring them back again afterwards, clean!'

'Yes, sir.'

'Don't call me "Sir". You call me "Corporal" or "Corp".'

'Yes, Corp.'

The meal was pretty bad, to tell the truth – rissoles and mash and mugs of steaming tea, which had a rather unusual taste. When I asked the corporal what it was he told me that it was bromide.

'Why?' I queried.

'To keep your mind off sex, of course.'

It was fascinating to find that it worked. If you wanted naughty thoughts at night or a good evening with a bird, you either had to abstain from cookhouse tea or buy it from the NAAFI. Egg and chips and a decent cup of unbromided tea cost only a shilling, but that was a fortune to us in C platoon; most of us came from very poor homes.

The first night was the worst for me – musty old blankets, no sheets, a hard bolster, iron camp beds on a hard concrete floor, with the two corporals sleeping on guard in little rooms either side of the door. But for many of the platoon this was undreamed-of luxury – three meals a day in hotel-like palaces. They quickly sorted out nicknames for each other. I was 'The Professor' – an acknowledgement that I could read and write and spoke with what they thought was a posh accent. Some of them asked me to write their letters home or to girlfriends, which was a little bit embarrassing. As Stan Laurel tells Oliver Hardy in *Beau Chumps* when he reads out Teeny Weeny's love letter, I tried not to listen as I wrote. It was nice to read to them the reply a week later – 'Darling . . . what a lovely letter, you have never written to me like that before. Army life must be doing you good.'

On the first full day we had our first basic lessons in drill, shambling a little better now to the officer's lecture which was about sex and the dangers of various activities, followed by a film show on the effects of VD. What was I getting myself into?

The following day, training began in earnest: PT, directed by the black-and-red-clothed instructors, fantastically fit and healthy, who had this motley bunch doing jumping and running exercises and threatened with even worse next morning, when there was to be a forced route-march. At least we did the PT in plimsolls – the route-march was to be in boots.

'How far?' I asked. (I was quickly elected spokesman.)

'A hundred miles' was the answer.

We all quaked in our plimsolls. Then into boots for drill by the sergeant, who threatened us with murder if we let him down in the competition to be top platoon of three in our six-week period.

'The leading person in each platoon gets a special award.' All eyes turned to me.

'Face front!'

So they tried to fashion us into a dreaded fighting unit in six weeks. If we reached a decent standard of dress and deportment by the end of the fourth week we could have an evening in Devizes, so we all tried our best.

C platoon evenutally won the competition (everyone was stood a cup of tea in the NAAFI) and I won the leading soldier competition. The prize was a bit of a let-down – an evening meal of anything I liked in the NAAFI – double egg and chips. We had to go before a selection board to decide what the army was going to do with us.

'What was your last job? . . . Oh, well, you could become a clerk. But I see you were in the JTC at school – why don't you try for a commission? If you want to go into the infantry you would enjoy the six-month course at the 28th Training Brigade at Palace Barracks, Holywood.'

My ears pricked up again, as I remembered *Beau Chumps* again:

'Number! One, two, three . . .' until they got to Stan Laurel. 'Come, come, my man, what is your number?'

'Hollywood.'

So the die was cast.

By coincidence, I recently did a BBC *Antiques Road-show* for children – 'The Next Generation' – just a mile away from Palace Barracks, and I walked down to look at the home where I lived for six months. It hasn't changed a bit, though there is now much more security and defences, because back in 1946 there was not the tension that has developed since. The camp was then the headquarters of the Irish Guards and they were put in charge of our drill. Life was much tougher than at Devizes. Everything was geared to make us fine infantrymen and future leaders of men. There were lads in most of the great British line regiments. The most fascinating were a bunch of Welsh boys who all sang, and we formed a small choir singing Welsh songs in harmony and in Welsh. I learned more about life, humanity and myself in those six months than in the rest of my life. We trained hard, went on dreadful route-marches and had map-reading training from a sergeant who knew less about the subject than we did, as we had all had been members of our school JTCs. I remember the map-reading lesson: 'There are two kinds of maps, big maps and little maps; big maps is miles to the inch and little maps is inches to the mile.' Then we were expected to put that into practice by being driven twenty miles into the countryside, dropped off in groups and making our way back to the camp, keeping clear of roads and avoiding patrols.

It wasn't all work and no play. We were allowed to go on a penny ride on the tram for miles the other side of Belfast to a military club where I spent happy hours playing their only decent gramophone record – the first act of Mozart's *Cosi fan Tutte*. I can close my eyes now and hear again the wonderful overture and opening trio. The Ulster people were terribly friendly and with a colleague I used to play in the weekly whist drives in Holywood. We won first prize in the Christmas drive – a fine goose – and a lovely local couple said they would cook it for us if we came to them for dinner on Christmas Day. Imagine our horror, when we got to the house, to be told that the cat had pinched the goose from the larder, so we shared a chicken instead.

The last couple of months of training were intense and led to the selection board in Edinburgh. This involved a weekend in comparative luxury – real food and sheets – but with the knowledge that you were being watched all the time and appraised: does he know how to use a knife and fork? We were an interesting, mixed bunch, some National Service, some regulars, all trying to become commissioned. We each had to give a short lecture – I chose the street names of London. Then came the mental and physical tests that had me in a panic, especially when I was presented with a nasty problem to solve. I had to get my group of eight across a deep circular pit, with a small island in the middle, using a couple of planks and pieces of rope, without touching the area around the island, which was declared mined, and with the enemy on the other side. There must have been a way of solving it but I couldn't see it. I got a couple of my team onto the middle island, where they remained like stranded whales for five minutes until my time was up – a complete failure. I went back to Palace Barracks convinced that I had not done well enough and when I was called into the CO's office to be told that I had not passed, I was resigned to my fate.

I was posted to Shorncliffe in Kent, a holding barracks intended for postings on to Germany. I was put into a reception office, booking in soldiers who arrived at the barracks after hours finding that this involved an almost certain weekend pass home, I wangled a permanent appointment. To be honest, I was not a very good soldier, and quickly found ways of skiving out of doing duties. The night I was put on guard of the coal dump, the camp lost most of the coal because squaddies kept on turning up with buckets pleading to be allowed to fill them up and take them back to their huts. I hadn't the heart to refuse. I joined the choir which sang in the garrison church, and helped out one of the Education Corps sergeants who found my musical achievements useful. We gave recitals at the camp and in the local villages, which the CO thought was good for public relations and for persuading the public that the licentious soldiery were not as bad as they were painted. I sang a few songs and the sergeant played the piano and we struck it off so well that he put me in for the army music and drama competitions that were held in Middlesex. I was entered for the baritone solo, which comprised *The Vagabond* by Ralph Vaughan Williams, and a free choice. This was my first music competition and I won, which led to a call on CO's orders, when I received congratulations.

That was nice – well, apart from the stupidity of the parade, when the regimental sergeant major marches you in and out of the office at double speed and you have to look your best – but it led to something that was to have quite an effect on my future life.

I was asked by Major O'Dell if I would join the South Eastern Command Concert Party and Shorncliffe Players, which were being formed to entertain the troops and civilians in the South East counties of Kent, Sussex and Surrey. One week there was a play and the next week a concert party and I was put into both. This got me out of virtually all army duties, though I remember in one play, which I was stage managing, there had to be a gun shot and I used my rifle to fire a blank. Imagine my horror when, next morning, Major Nolda, the new Company Commander, called a sudden parade as he thought we were all terribly sloppy. (He sounded just like Terry-Thomas – 'You're an absolute shower!') An inspection of rifles found the barrel of mine absolutely filthy from the powder of the blank. So instead of weekend leave I had extra drill. How I hated Major Nolda!

I had better luck with the concert party. I was the resident baritone, singing songs such as *Glorious Devon*. All I can say is that the concert was just a little better than that wonderful army concert party in the BBC series *It Ain't 'Arf 'Ot, Mum!* But an extraordinary thing happened some forty-five years later, after I had shown a slide on TV in a programme commemorating fifteen years of the *Antiques Roadshow*. I was amazed to get a letter from Ken Passey, the compère of the concert party, saying that he had recognised himself and we met again after all that time. I was shocked to see that he had aged – apparently some people do – though I looked just the same, of course.

The experience of singing in public gave me the confidence to determine to go into the profession in some form when I left the army.

On the day of my release, I received my demob suit, clothes and pork pie hat, and travelled home to my parents, who had moved to a council flat in Marshall Street in Soho, near Carnaby Street. I had been given three weeks' demob leave, during which time I was still technically in the army. I discovered that if I wore my uniform and went to the forces centre in Leicester Square I could obtain pairs of free theatre tickets, given to help fill seats. My mother and I went to a large number of West End shows to see some of the great actors of the time in memorable plays, so the end of my army career was happier than the start. But I had to start back into human life.

I restarted at St Paul's Cathedral Sunday Evening Choir, but received a bad put-down when the boy choristers laughed at my pork pie hat, which I was proudly wearing. 'Where did you get that hat?' they jeered, and on my way home I threw the hat into the first bomb site I passed. I rejoined the Alexandra Choir and the conductor, Charles Proctor, suggested I had lessons from Topliss Green, who had been a famous baritone in his day. He took me on and I went to his studio once a week.

I restarted work at the NBM in the Fire Department, working with Herbert Till, who had returned from war service while I was doing National Service. He was the producer of the Newland Players and suggested that I applied for the NBM operatic society production of *Véronique* by André Messager. I attended the auditions and was given the leading male part. I seem to have made a success of the part and the following year was offered the part of the Earl of Essex in Edward German's *Merrie England*. This was a fine musical score and I enjoyed it very much.

The NBM clerical job was not very highly paid and my musical education was costing a fair bit. There were singing lessons with Topliss Green, purchase of a lot of music and attending recitals and concerts. I even rented a phone to take requests for engagements, and had cards printed. These began to bear fruit when a quartet engaged me as the bass for performing at weddings and funerals at churches where they had no resident choir, such as All Souls, Langham Place, at the top of Regent Street near the BBC. We would sometimes get two a day, at a guinea a head each time, which was nice for a half-hour service. The music seemed to be the same for a wedding as for a funeral: Crimond ('The Lord's My Shepherd') and *Jesu, Joy of Man's Desiring*. These West End society weddings fascinated me as the same flower arrangements were used for as many services as there were that day, but each bridal party was charged afresh each time. One church used to play a record of bells from the bell tower at the end of the service and at the end of one wedding, as the quartet filed out, we heard the tolling of the funeral bell – *Bong! . . . Bong!* The verger had put the wrong side of the record on. I never did find out what happened to him.

I sang on Sunday mornings in a double quartet, at the City church of St Edmund King and Martyr, for twenty-six guineas per annum. The singers were semi-professionals and the standard was high, though there was no congregation to speak of. No one lived in the City, of course, and the only congregation you could expect was the occasional visitor to different churches and the rector's mother. The choir used to sit down in the nave during the sermon to make a congregation and although the sermons were pretty poor, usually about the life of St Edmund, I did enjoy the singing. One of the settings that was a particular favourite of the organist was Edgar Day in B flat, and when I went to Worcester Cathedral and found that Edgar was assistant organist there I was delighted to meet him. He in turn was delighted to learn that I used to sing in St Edmund's choir, as his setting was always appearing in *The Times'* list of music being sung on Sundays. It was the only place apart from Worcester where it was being done at that time.

At St Paul's Cathedral on Sunday evenings, Ron Alexander, Michael Vaile, David Johnston and I formed a quartet, singing for our own enjoyment. We called ourselves the Cathedral Singers, and we were joined by three fine young sopranos that I met at the church of St Martin in the Fields – Helen Harley, Margaret Barker and Jane Callow. The seven of us gave a lot of recitals, some conducted by the organist of St Martin's, John Churchill. We did a number of concerts with the Croydon Youth Orchestra, singing works such as Handel's Chandos Anthems, and that gave all of us the experience of singing with an orchestra. David Johnston was later to become a professional tenor famous in oratorio and opera, although he did many of our concerts when he should have been at home studying to be an accountant. One concert at a church in Croydon caused us a lot of worry. In the first half we should have sung the Chandos Anthem No. 6, *Oh Praise the Lord with One Consent*, but there was no sign of David. So the Handel anthem was postponed to the end of the second half and we all waited outside the church. Finally, ten minutes before the deadline, there was a distant figure galloping down the road and David arrived. He was out of breath, but recovered in time to perform splendidly.

I was still having lessons from Topliss Green, who thought it good for me to go in for music competitions. Most areas of London held them and it was certainly a good training to compete in the bass or baritone classes, judged critically by leading adjudicators such as the composers Herbert Howells and Michael Head. I gained a number of prizes – not money, but medals and certificates – but set my sights on the Sutton and Cheam Music Festival, which had an open class for a recitative and aria in which the prize was the Martin Attwater Exhibition, giving a year's tuition at the Guildhall School of Music. This was adjudicated by Helen Henshall and involved

two rounds; the first reduced the fifty-odd competitors to six, who then went into the final and sang
a recitative and aria from Handel's *Messiah*, 'The
people that walked in darkness'. I thought I had done
quite well, but there was a brilliant young soprano
also in the final and when Helen said that she had
had a difficult job choosing between the two of us,
there were at least two hearts in the mouth. Then
Helen said that the prize was going to the older one –
me – as the younger soprano had years ahead of her
to try again.

The Guildhall School of Music was a quick half-
mile walk from the North British office, and the
weekly singing lessons were on a weekday, which
meant that I either had to slip out or get official
permission. Harold Rattle suggested that I slipped
out and Herbert Till thought I should ask permission
from the department head, saying that it would be a
big help for my future performances with the operatic
society. Being a coward I did the latter, so once a
week, for a year, off I went through the front door
with official blessing. I had been put to Walter Hyde,
then a very old man but in his youth a famous
operatic tenor, who had achieved pre-war fame in the
great Wagnerian roles in English at Covent Garden.
His voice was still magnificent and I was in awe as
he was able to sail up to top Cs in an effortless way.
He was a very inspiring teacher, although his piano
playing was not terribly good and he accompanied
my singing in a way that put me off. I mentioned this

to Harold Rattle and he remembered being assistant organist at a London church when Walter Hyde sang in the choir back in the 1920s. He suggested coming along to meet the professor and playing for me at a lesson. We did this without prior agreement and I must admit that I got told off, although Mr Hyde was interested in being reminded about the old days. I only did this the once and at the end of the first term Walter Hyde died. His pupils were put to other professors and mine was Arthur Reckless, whose fine baritone was more like my voice, which had developed into a bass-baritone. My new teacher was an oratorio singer and broadcaster, and we forged a close link when he found that I had already gained the ARCM diploma. He put me in for a number of concerts for which he was asked to provide a promising pupil, and I had the joy of having him sing for me in *The Messiah* with the choral society that I conducted when I went to Worcester.

Gaining the diploma of Associate of the Royal College of Music was a proud moment. I was helped in preparing for it by John Churchill, the organist of St Martin in the Fields, with whom I struck up a great friendship, and it is sad that he has (only recently) died. John, or Jack as he was generally known, had only just been appointed to the post and built up a good mixed-voice choir to sing a cathedral-type choral evensong on a Sunday afternoon and, expanded, large-scale choral works with orchestra. This was a great innovation at St Martin's, which had been a very low church, but the new Vicar, Rev. Charles-Edwards, and his wife, who was a fine musician, gave Jack great encouragement to develop the musical power of the church. He gathered around him some splendid musicians. He gave me enormous help and encouragement, allowing me to sing the solos in big works such as Mozart's Requiem and to give three recitals in the Tuesday lunchtime series. These gave me quite a big exposure and some impressive press notices. In particular, he coached me in theory and composition for the ARCM exam (he taught at the Royal College) and accompanied me at a coming-out recital.

The clerical job at the NBM was getting stultifying, and I felt I had to go full time into music, though I knew that it was a difficult profession. So I watched out for an interesting post and one appeared in the *Musical Times* – a vacancy for a bass lay clerk in the choir of Worcester Cathedral. My parents thought it was a good idea, especially as Worcester was only a hundred miles away from home and they wouldn't lose me to the Outer Hebrides. So I applied and had a lovely letter from David Willcocks, the organist and choirmaster, inviting me to go to Worcester for an interview and audition one Sunday morning in 1953.

As the train went through the beautiful countryside of Worcestershire, my nose was pressed against the window – was that really Bredon Hill that I used to sing about in the many settings of the wonderful poem by A. E. Housman? Were those the Malvern

Hills, so beloved of Edward Elgar? David Willcocks met me at the station (he had rushed through the morning services to get there) and drove me to the fascinating organist's house in College Green to have lunch with his family. Then he had me sing something in the cathedral, we had an interview with the Dean and they offered me the post, to commence at the start of the summer term, just before Coronation Day. I was told that the stipend was a miserably low figure of £170 per annum, paid quarterly (Willcocks had had it raised from £120 only a year before by reducing the number of full-time lay clerks from eight to six), but there were other fees, such as those for the Three Choirs Festival, occasional broadcasts and special services. Also he thought that he could get me some teaching at the Royal Grammar School, as he was impressed with the ARCM, even though that was a performing and not a teaching diploma.

I attended Evensong in the organ loft and I found that Willcocks was something of a showman. He showed me the periscope that his predecessor, Sir Ivor Atkins, used to observe the choir, while Willcocks would rip the curtain aside and shout and grimace. The small organ loft was crowded with visitors and at the end of the service Willcocks said, 'Who is the youngest?' A teenage girl raised her hand. 'Well, you can choose the voluntary. What's it to be?' She stuttered out a particular toccata and fugue by Bach, and Willcocks played it with a great flourish and from memory. The admiring crowd buzzed with

joy, until there came into the loft Sir Ivor Atkins himself, an ancient and famous musician, who held the
record for the longest period as Worcester organist.
The atmosphere changed instantly and I realised that
Willcocks was in awe of his predecessor. At the end
of the fugue, Sir Ivor (or Saliva, as the choristers used
to call him) said, 'Can't you span a tenth, Willcocks?'

'No, Sir Ivor,' came the reply. (Willcocks had
remarkably small hands.)

'Well, I can.' And Sir Ivor proved it.

Willcocks introduced me to Atkins and I did quite
well by saying that I admired his editions of early
music, for which he was well known. I was driven
back to the station and told to report at the start of
term.

I served out a month's notice at the North British. I
said goodbye to everyone with many regrets, for I
knew I could not push a pen for the next forty-odd
years. The last week was spent in the British Museum
Reading Room, copying out a marvellous score by
Maurice Greene entitled *The Judgment of Paris*, which
I had the idea of editing and performing. I also edited
a number of anthems by Thomas Tomkins, organist
of Worcester in the seventeenth century. Then I said a
fond farewell to my parents and my many musical
friends and set off for my new life in Worcester.

4

Worcester Music-Making

On arrival in Worcester, I stayed with the Stevensons, who rented a cathedral flat in the old coachhouse that was in the grounds of the old Bishop's Palace, a quick fifty-yard dash from the cathedral. Cyril Stevenson had been a tenor lay clerk in Salisbury Cathedral but moved to Worcester when David Willcocks became organist of Salisbury. When Willcocks followed Atkins at Worcester, poor Stevenson was demoted to supernumerary to reduce the cost of stipends. So Cyril only sang at weekends, whereas the full-time lay clerks sang Monday evensong, Tuesday morning practice and evensong, Thursday mattins, Friday morning litany and evensong, plus Saturday morning practice and evensong and three services on Sunday. (They had dropped Monday morning mattins just before I arrived, as it had been pointed out that the employers where you worked first on Monday were responsible for paying your National Insurance and Health stamps.) The morning services had been moved from 10.30 to 8.30 and the evening services had been moved from 4.00 to 5.15 to enable the lay clerks to fit in another job. Cyril Stevenson gave me lots of interesting tidbits of information about the cathedral and my colleagues, so I was ready for the next day's mattins at the horribly early time of 8.30 a.m.

I was first into the lay clerks' vestry and waited a long time for the next arrival. I could hear old Mr Nicholls ('Chick' to his friends) coming panting up the turret stairs a couple of minutes before I saw him. He was the oldest lay clerk, an alto with a very sweet, pure voice which was sometimes a bit out of tune, to the chagrin of Willcocks, who was blessed (or cursed) with a sense of perfect pitch and anything slightly out of tune must have been agony. Chick Nicholls' main job was as Clerk to the Kings School, at which the cathedral choristers had their education. He had been a noted dance-band player in his youth and had had his own band, but that was back in the 1920s and 30s. He was not too keen on authority – he had rows with Sir Ivor Atkins, who when he met Chick in the cloisters would say something like, 'Good morning, Nicholls.'

'Is it?' would come the reply.

Chick was technically senior lay clerk, but did not fancy the task and delegated his duty to the next arrival in the vestry, Victor Dowse.

Victor Dowse was my bass oppo, singing on Cantoris side while I sang on Decani (the side where the Dean's stall was). Victor was a great character – an Irishman who had sung in St Patrick's Cathedral, Dublin, before coming to Worcester. He had worked for the Ministry of Food during the war, then became

My grandparents' Golden Wedding Anniversary. They are seated in front with Bob.
Behind are some of their children – from left to right: Rosie, Vera,
Dora, Lionel, Ruby, Clara (my mother) and Leslie.

Bob and my father in the silent film *Scrags –The Tale of a Dog*, 1928.
My father played the tramp and I was in the film as a baby.

Bob's birthday tea party, 1929. Sharing his party are, from left to right:
me, my cousins Ronald and Sylvia (children of Reg and Elsie) and the son of
Charlie Kunz (the pianist whose signature tune was 'Clap hands,
here comes Charlie'). Photograph © Fox Photos

Bob and me 'busking' in Newport Buildings, Soho, where we lived, 1932.
The violin was made for me by Grandpa. Still from a film © Fox Photos

Monty Banks directing my father and me in a film, 1932. Bob II is trying to save me
from being kidnapped. Monty Banks was a famous actor and film producer, and
married Gracie Fields. Photograph © Fox Photos

Me with Bob II, a popular postcard of the 1930s.

John Justin as the blind beggar in *The Thief of Baghdad* with Bob II by his side and being addressed by my father, 1939. The scene was shot in Denham Studios.
Photograph © National Film Archive

The Amazing Doctor Clitterhouse, a High Wycombe Royal Grammar School play in which I played Nurse Ann, 1941.

A photograph of me by my aunt Vivienne at her 20th Century Studios in
Hamilton Mews, Piccadilly, 1944. She could make anyone look handsome.

National Service primary training at Devizes, 1946.
I am in the back row, on the far left.

The South East Command Concert Party at Shorncliffe Camp, Kent, 1947.
I was the resident baritone (the shorter one wearing a dicky-bow in the photo).
Standing beside me is the compere Ken Passey. Among the other members were
the comedian George Cox, the accordionist Pat Murphy and the producer
Major O'Dell (who is kneeling in the bottom right of the photo).

As the Earl of Essex in the North British and Mercantile Operatics
production of *Merrie England*, with Jessie Parker as Queen Elizabeth the First, 1950.
I am probably one of the few people who have met both Queen Elizabeth
the First and Queen Elizabeth the Second.

Worcester Cathedral Choir, 1957. Seated in the second row, from left to right, are: me, Neville Dilks, Victor Dowse, the assistant organist Edgar Day, the Minor Canon, Dean Milburn, the organist Douglas Guest, Llechid Williams, Ben Choyce and Captain Kirkby. Standing behind in the centre are, from left to right: Hugh Watson, Denis Wickens, Anthony Hayward and Malcolm Darling. Among the choristers are some who have become famous musicians.

As Music Master of Worcester Royal Grammar School, 1954.

On our wedding day outside Worcester Cathedral, 1956.
From left to right: Barbara's father, Judith (Barbara's niece, who was bridesmaid),
Barbara's mother, Barbara, my father, me, my mother and Bob Mirkellian
(an old army mate who was my best man).

'Allo, allo, allo, what have we got here?' A Roman skull
from our garden near the Cathedral, 1957.

Chapter Clerk to the cathedral, having a little office in College Yard from which he made his occasional forays to Chapter meetings in the Chapter House and to sing in the choir. He smoked Passing Clouds cigarettes and was a great drinker – not the black stuff of Ireland but things such as 'gin and It', which he kept in his safe. He could see anyone approaching his office through his window and there would be a clinking of bottles and glasses hurriedly being hidden away and when you entered he would be all beaming smiles, behind a smokescreen of Passing Clouds, with piles of papers all over the huge desk, showing that he was very busy. He acted as senior lay clerk and took this position very seriously, if somewhat pompously, being a little like Toad in *Wind in the Willows*. His best days as a singer had gone and his higher notes were difficult for him, so when there was a high solo verse he would give a nod in my direction and I would sing it for him. He insisted that he paid me £10 per annum, paid quarterly, to do this, saying that when he came to Worcester the old bass then – Smith – did the same for him, so I agreed. He told me that he regarded himself as the father of the choir, so I coined the title 'Daddy Dowse' for him and everyone called him that.

The senior tenor was a Welshman, Llechid Williams. He had a fine Welsh tenor voice and I used him in many concerts of mine and sang with him in smoking concerts when we would do great Victorian duets, such as *Excelsior*. He was quite convinced that Wales

was the greatest place in the world and I used to tell
him that was rubbish. When we sang the solo parts
in Haydn's *Creation* and I stood up to sing the great
bass recitative 'And God created great whales',
Llechid nudged me in the ribs and said, 'There you
are, boyo, I told you so.' He had a fiery temper and
was always having battles with Daddy Dowse,
especially getting cross when Daddy came down
from his stall to conduct the choir in an unaccompanied anthem, whereas it should have been
done by wagging a finger from the stalls, mirrored
by the senior on the other side. Llechid's other job
was as a clerk at Kay's mail-order firm, the largest
employer in Worcester.

The tenor oppo on Cantoris was Neville Dilks, who
was the English master at the King's School. His
initials on school timetables were NED so, of course,
to all the boys and to us he was Ned. Ned was a
lovely man. An expert in the English language, he
was always being called upon by Willcocks when he
was going through the psalms for the day at practice,
to get the correct meaning of the beautiful words.
Ned had a great love of cricket and football and acted
as our expert to pick the draws for our football pool
entries. He had a wonderful sense of humour, with
an incredible ability to come out with a devastating
pun. He had come to Worcester from Leicester
Cathedral, and had two brilliantly academic sons
who went to Worcester Royal Grammar School (one
became a professor of political history at Leeds Uni-

versity). His wife taught at the convent school in Worcester, so, as you can imagine, I was a bit in awe of the family.

The younger oppo to Chick Nicholls was also a teacher – Malcolm Darling. He taught at a small preparatory boys' school, Hawford Lodge, but when the school expanded he found it a big problem to fit this in with the cathedral. He was a godson of David Willcocks and taught maths, art and pottery as well as taking games, so his time was full. He was happy when a full-time replacement was found and he could become a part-time supernumerary. His knowledge of maths was amazing to me and during the sermon he would work out a complicated algebraic or geometric equation, which left me mesmerised. He became a fine amateur potter, taking lessons from Geoffrey Whiting, as I did, and produced a superb jug decorated with one of Edgar Day's psalm tunes; we presented it to Edgar when he retired. Many years later, after Edgar's death, I found the jug in a local junk shop and was able to buy it and give it to my son David, who prizes it enormously.

There were three supernumeraries who augmented the six full-time lay clerks at weekends. Ben Choyce was the bass, a big, gentle man who travelled for an oil firm and sang by Daddy Dowse. The tenor was Cyril Stevenson, a Devonian with a pronounced burr. He was a master baker and came out with some risqué jokes. After we sang the Boyce verse anthem *O Where shall Wisdom be Found?*, in which the price of wisdom is said to be beyond the price of rubies, he would say, 'But they never tell us what was Ruby's price'. The most fascinating supernumerary was the alto, Captain Kirkby. He was a retired naval captain and I think he had been in charge of stores at Portsmouth or somewhere, never having gone to sea in anger. As a spare-time and low-paid job he looked after the choir music, skilfully sewing the music into brown paper folders and repairing damage caused by generations of choristers' fingers. Captain Kirkby had a very short fuse and especially hated long sermons, which he managed to cut off in their prime by blowing his nose very loudly, sounding just like a foghorn at sea. His was a male alto voice, unlike the natural countertenor voice which Peter Salmon had. Kirkby's voice had a change of gear from the head voice to the chest voice and when I took over the duties of librarian after his death it was fascinating to see in his music copies arrows pointing to certain notes and 'Change gear here' written boldly.

The choir sang at the wedding of Canon Braley's daughter and we went to the reception afterwards in College Hall. Most of the men had a goodly amount to drink and Kirkby more than most. At the evensong later in the day, Kirkby turned to Llechid Williams during the first lesson and said, very loudly, 'What's next?' Llechid answered *sotto voce* something which I did not hear but I am sure that everybody in the cathedral heard Kirkby's reply:

'Christ, I've already sung that!'

Willcocks was always prepared to bring in a good singer to sing with the choir on a temporary basis. He kindly allowed David Johnston, who had sung with the Cathedral Singers in London, to join the choir at weekends while he was in the navy and studying Russian translation at an inland naval station in Wythall, south of Birmingham. David stayed with me in the Bishop's Coach House – the Old Lodge Flat as we called it. After Cyril Stevenson died I took over the lease and Mrs Stevenson stayed on as house-keeper until she went to run a post office stores in North Worcester.

David Willcocks was a brilliant and mercurial musician. Awarded the Military Cross in the war, he ran a very tight ship in the cathedral. He could be difficult to deal with as a professional, expecting things to be perfect, as of course they should be in a professional choir. But he had taken over a rather ancient choir from Sir Ivor Atkins and not all of them were really up to it at their age. They had joined the choir on what was called 'the Foundation', which gave them the post for life tenure, unless they committed a serious misdemeanour. I never knew how serious this had to be, as no one knew of anyone in the past who had been given the push. I was told the story of Samuel Sebastian Wesley, the composer and organist of half a dozen churches, upsetting Deans and Chapters all over the place. He ended up at Hereford Cathedral where, after one altercation, the Dean and Chapter gave him the sack. He said he couldn't be sacked because he was on the Foundation; he took them to the High Court and the judge ruled for him. At the next Sunday service he is said to have put down as the introit, 'How dear are thy counsels unto me, O Lord'; the hymn, 'The church's one foundation'; and the anthem by Handel, *Fixed in his everlasting seat*. I should have been on the Foundation but Daddy Dowse never got round to drawing up the document.

I always thought of Willcocks as an incredible character like Wesley. Outside the cathedral he was incredibly dashing, able to entertain at the piano like a music-hall artist. He could sit on the floor, back to the piano, and play by raising his hands backwards over his shoulders. He would go through a cathedral service singing all the verses in the style of the different lay clerks, and when he did Kirkby's gear change he had everyone in stitches. But in the cathedral it was a deadly serious business. Friday morning litany, which the choir sang unaccompanied, was actually accompanied by Willcocks going round the nave and whenever he heard a wrong note or bad tuning, he would kick a chair, which made a frightening noise. He shared my love of the psalms and was a brilliant interpreter of them on the organ. You could hear the birds singing and the quails quailing. The plagues in Egypt brought out the best in him, with frogs croaking and lice scratching you in all your quarters. My favourite verse was 'But when I said, My foot hath slipt'; he had the curtain pulled aside and I could see his face wreathed in smiles as he let his foot slide over the pedals. The cathedral choir did a demonstration to a group of organists and choirmasters and he showed them how to train a choir, getting us to sing badly, out of tune or something, then show how to improve it. 'How do you get a choir to sing "Amen" together?' he was asked. Easy: 'A – men,' we sang perfectly together, to applause. He showed how to measure perfectly the singing of Anglican chants, unlike the usual gabble in a church of a rush up to the first barline and then a slow slog. He had a bit of fun by changing the barlines of the wonderful verse, 'Grin like a dog and / go a/bout the / city' to 'Grin like a dog a go a / bow wow/ wought the / city.'

He was at his best when he rehearsed and conducted the choral society, who sang concerts of their own in the cathedral. A contingent of the best of them also joined the best of Hereford and Gloucester choral societies in the wonderful Three Choirs Festival, the oldest provincial music festival in the world, held annually in each of the three cities in turn since the late seventeenth century. In my first year – 1953 – it was the turn of Gloucester, whose organist was Dr Sumsion, who chose the works for the week and was the main conductor, though the other two organists – David Willcocks and Meredith Davies of Hereford – conducted their share. Willcocks was brilliant with an amateur chorus, lively, exciting and humorous, always ready to come out with an amusing story to

make a point. To get over the correct way of pro-
nouncing *Ah* instead of a short *A* in a Latin piece he
would hold up proceedings and tell of a French car
driver who flagged down a motorist in a Worcestershire lane and asked him, 'Where is the Ah Ah?'

'Oh, you'll have to go behind the tree – there isn't
one near here.'

'Non, le Ah Ah!'

This story went on for five minutes until the
Worcestershire man realised that it was the AA that
was wanted. I'm sure none of the chorus got the
sound wrong after that. The choral societies idolised
him, and I learned a lot about the techniques of choral
conducting just from watching him.

He was of enormous help to me. As well as recom-
mending me to the Royal Grammar School as music
master, he gave me some concerts in the Worcester
Festival Choral Society's seasons, notably two performances of Bach's St Matthew Passion in which I
sang all the different characters – Peter, Pilate etc. It
was an enormous thrill to stand on the platform in
morning suit in a line-up of soloists that was the
equivalent of being in the forward line with
Matthews and Finney or the Middlesex team with
Compton and Edrich. There was Eric Greene as the
Evangelist and John Carol Case as the Christus. Eric
Greene was rightly regarded as the finest interpreter
of the difficult role of the Evangelist and it was
fascinating looking at his vocal score in which he had
written all the different rhythms used at different

places. How he kept his eye on the right line for Worcester I will never know. We, of course, used the edition prepared by Elgar and Atkins – how could Worcester do anything else?

The assistant organist of Worcester Cathedral was Edgar Day and I have no hesitation in saying that he was the loveliest person I have ever met: sweet-tempered, kind and gentle. If the Church of England could have made someone a saint he would have been the first. When I arrived at Worcester he already held the record as the longest-serving assistant organist in the history of English cathedral music, happy in the somewhat lowly position in music to which God had appointed him. Nowadays a promising organist takes a position as assistant in anticipation of it being a stepping stone to becoming organist of a cathedral, gradually rising up the ladder. Edgar had been the articled pupil to Atkins before the first world war, had a rather bad time while serving in France and after the war was appointed assistant organist. For years he looked after his brother, who had what we would now term Down's Syndrome; he also taught music at the King's School, trained the probationer choristers, acted as accompanist to the choral society, played the organ for services and was assistant to Atkins, Willcocks and Douglas Guest in turn, until he finally retired. He was a fine composer, whether the music was for the cathedral service, such as his wonderful setting of the canticles in B flat, now a cornerstone of many cathedrals, or many fine anthems such as *Round me falls the Night*; or secular pieces such as a riotous and difficult setting of *Hey Diddle Diddle*.

Edgar became a firm friend of Sir Edward Elgar, the Worcester-born Master of the King's Musick, and every now and then would come up with a wonderful story, told in a shy and unboastful way that was typical of him. After a Three Choirs Festival concert they had been to a buffet party at a house a couple of miles to the north of Worcester. When the time came, Elgar asked Edgar if he would walk back to the city with him. Elgar was silent all the way, deep in thought, and Edgar did not want to disturb the great man. Lord knows what great compositions were forming in his mind. Finally when they had almost reached Elgar's house on Rainbow Hill, he spoke: 'Edgar, didn't you think that ham was rather salty?'

I learned from Edgar Day how different was the way cathedral music was performed in Edwardian days, much slower and more stately. If he played the organ for a service when the organist was away, a piece such as Blair in B minor sounded like a different work. Obviously he had been born into a more stately and gracious age and yet he was fully prepared to forget his own thoughts and beliefs and obey his master. Willcocks idolised him and they played a weekly game of golf. Occasionally Edgar was made to conduct one of his own anthems and he would shyly appear by the side of the choir, looking awkward in a cassock and surplice without a doctor's diploma hood, as he never received any such honour.

The choristers loved him but used to play him up when he had to take a rehearsal and especially when he trained the probationers, which was done in the cathedral round an old piano, while the full choristers rehearsed in the Chapter House. Howard Briggs, who was the finest treble that I ever sang with, told me that one of the probationers would hide in the font and make groaning noises every now and then; or they would jam piano notes with bits of toast from breakfast so that the rehearsal had to be abandoned. Choristers can be tough and difficult. They are chosen because they are lively and confident and they lead a very hard life, having to fit in school work with all their singing duties, which were much heavier then than they are now. But they got an enormous amount out of their chorister's training, learning skills in music, deportment, speech and concentration which are invaluable to them in later years. They can see through a phoney and make his life miserable, as can schoolboys, of course.

I found out from Howard Briggs that we all had nicknames. I was instantly christened 'Arthur Crosby'.

'Why?' I wanted to know.

'Because you look like Arthur Askey and sing like Bing Crosby' was the answer.

Howard sang like a little angel, but was a naughty boy, in danger of getting expelled many times. He would turn up for a service with his arm in a sling having broken it for some reason or other.

I remember his last service. I persuaded Willcocks to do the marvellous anthem *Hear My Prayer*, with the next section 'Oh for the wings of a dove'. I got the local paper to publicise it and a huge crowd turned up, instead of the usual 'two or three gathered together'. There was not a dry eye in the place when this fantastic voice soared up to heaven and no one who was there will ever forget it.

I was amazed at how few people attended the services. Obviously you couldn't expect many to come at 8.30 in the morning and usually we just sang to the glory of God, as perfectly as we could. A weekday evensong was not much better attended, although there was a big crowd on Sundays, especially at mattins, which was held in the nave when the local boarding schools had compulsory attendance. At evensong we had some regular fans, who almost fought for their favourite seats. I was a bit frightened of a pair of maiden sisters, the Misses Robinson, who I thought had designs on me. They wore pointed hats, stood behind me, smiling secret smiles when I used to find a special present on my stall – a punnet of raspberries in season or a bag of sweets. They wanted me to go and stay with them in their house in Bath Road and I wouldn't agree. Well, I had just come down from London where I had seen the film *Arsenic and Old Lace* and I thought that a fate would befall me similar to that which befell the poor souls in the film. Years later I found out that the Misses Robinson had looked after the great Royal Worcester artist Richard Seabright until he died and I felt rather sad that I had not taken up their offer.

Directly responsible for the religious aspect of the choral services was the Precentor, who was Rev. Desmond Pocock. He got on very well with the choir, especially the choristers, and I saw how important a position this was when he left the cathedral to take a living in Hampshire: he was succeeded by several Precentors who were not so good, and the Dean and Chapter persuaded Desmond to return.

The running of a cathedral is in the hands of a Dean and usually four canons in residence. Dean Beck was not a well man; he had had an operation on his head and had to wear a skull cap, but he was still going strong and able to marry us in 1956.

The canons were an interesting bunch. Canon Shepherd was Vice-Dean and a bit of a dry stick. Ned Dilks told me that Shepherd once stopped Sir Ivor Atkins after a number of anthems by the long-dead Worcester organist Thomas Tomkins had been sung. 'Tell me,' he asked, 'is this Tomkins still composing?'

'No, Canon,' came the answer. 'He is decomposing.'

Canon Briggs was a rather wizened old man who was always writing hymns – the words, not the music.

Canon Braley had been head of Durham theological college before coming to Worcester and we discovered that his students would say as their Lord's Prayer, 'Give us this day our Braley dead.' I think this was done in a kindly way, as he really was a very human and amusing person, a bit like the sporting and drinking clergyman in a Trollope novel. He was the cathedral appointee to the country cricket club, as the Dean and Chapter owned the ground at the time.

The fourth canon was Claude Armstrong, who was very scholarly and aesthetic and as likely to address you in Latin or Greek as in English. He was head of the Worcester theological college, which sought to train elderly and retired men for the ministry, and I am sure he had a great inner sense of humour to be able to do this.

I threw myself into the life of the cathedral but needed more income than was provided by my stipend. I applied for the post of music master at the Worcester Royal Grammar School for Boys and was accepted. This was a fine school, thought to be among the oldest in the country, having been founded by one of the Worcester saints, St Oswald, in Saxon days. The headmaster was Godfrey Brown, usually known by his initials A. G. K. Brown. He had been a great athlete in pre-war days, achieving a gold medal in the Berlin Olympic Games of 1936 for the quarter-mile relay. He was naturally very keen on sports and when he found a kindred spirit in me he was delighted. I told him that I liked cricket and had joined the Worcester rugby club, so I found that a number of my class music lessons were changed to taking forms for swimming – especially worrying when I could not swim a stroke. I was engaged to take the three forms of the first two years for weekly class lessons, plus coaching any of the boys who wished to take music in their examinations. The person nominally over me was A. T. Shaw, the art master, who was also a keen musician, organist and founder of the Elgar Society. He was especially keen on the works of Edward Elgar, in those days nowhere near as popular as they are now. He also conducted the school orchestra and put on regular concerts.

Not having been trained to be a schoolteacher, I naturally felt a bit of fear at taking my first classes, but the school had a strong sense of discipline, so although there were a few difficult boys I got through things reasonably well. There were certain things I had to do each lesson, such as teach them the hymns for the next week's school assembly, find out the better voices for the school choir and introduce them all to the works that were going to be performed. When we did Purcell's *Dido and Aeneas* in the Perrins Hall (built through the beneficence of Dyson Perrins, son of the founder of the Worcestershire Sauce firm of Lea and Perrins and also founder of the great collection of Worcester porcelain, of which I later became curator), we sang the echo chorus by having a group of boys go outside and sing the echo through the window. I introduced them to a lot of musical instruments that they could borrow for a week to torment their parents with and the boys that I coached would bring their instruments into the lessons to show how they worked. We ended up the first term by showing the film *The Instruments of the Orchestra*, introduced by Sir Malcolm Sargent, under whom I had sung in a 1,000-voice *Messiah* in the Royal Albert Hall.

I think the boys got a lot of fun and a certain amount of knowledge out of these lessons. To rub in points I instituted a system of blips and blops, pulling the hair and banging the head, but very gently of course, not to cause any physical injury (although in those days one was allowed to punish). It was intended to show the rhythm and I often meet ex-pupils who seem to remember the blips and blops with great affection. I think my greatest moment was with one boy who used to jiggle and joggle around whenever I put on a gramophone record. When I asked him why he did this, he would say, 'Because I like records, sir.' For the next lesson, I planted an old wax record in the music cupboard and when he started his jigging I called him out in front, asked him why did it and got the same answer, 'Because I like records, sir.' So I got the old record and hit him over the head with it. Little bits of the record flew every-where and the whole class was silent. When I had everyone's attention, I said to the boy himself, 'Now you can always tell your descendants that you once broke a school record.' Many years later I was walking along a Worcester street and had a tap on my shoulder. I turned round and looked up at the tallest policeman I had ever seen (and the Worcester police wore spikes on the top of their helmets, which made them appear even taller).

'You don't remember me, do you, sir?'

'No,' I said.

'I was the boy you hit on the head with a record.'

Quick as a flash, I told him that it didn't seem to have stunted his growth.

The second term we suffered an inspection by Her Majesty's Inspectorate. This was a worry to the school (and to me) as there had not been one for years, and I was told they were always very thorough. One of the inspectors came once into one of my classes and that was all.

The part of the teaching that I enjoyed the most was the coaching of boys for the exams and especially for university scholarships. It was particularly interesting working with young men and helping them, as I myself had been helped. A number became professional musicians but the one I was most proud of was David Parkes, who obtained a choral scholarship to St Catherine's College, Cambridge, helped by being allowed to sing with the cathedral choir at weekends.

My years at the Grammar School produced a number of interesting things. I became friends with Edgar Billingham, the English master, who had written some episodes for radio entitled *The Barchester Rovers*, about a Midlands football club. These were broadcast from Birmingham and used a number of the actors who played parts in *The Archers*. He hummed a theme tune to me to the words 'Up the Barchester Rovers' and I set it for a town brass band as a march, with the words sung by the cast. It was all great fun and ran for a number of weekly episodes, but regrettably not as long as *The Archers*. We also participated in the writing of a light opera based on the love affair of Elizabeth Barrett and Robert Browning, called *The Beauty of Bath*. We didn't get too far with it but I composed enough tunes to be able to give a lecture about it to the young ladies of Cheltenham Ladies' College. Edgar Billingham told the story and I sang the songs, accompanied by Trevor Protheroe, the Latin master at the RGS and organist of St John's church in Worcester.

I had taken over the St John's Choral Society from Llechid Williams, the tenor lay clerk. St John's is an area on the west side of the River Severn, opposite the cathedral, and the choir had been founded by Edward Elgar. During Llechid's time, the concerts were of the light operatic type – *A Tale of Old Japan*, or *The Rebel Maid* (in which I sang the lead). On taking over, I wanted to put on better concerts, in the Public Hall, a fine building in which many of Elgar's secular works had had their first performance. We kicked off with a performance of *The Messiah*, in the hope of making money from the old pot-boiler, but I freshened the work up by introducing some solos that were not usually done, and by using a small choir and orchestra. This was thought rather revolutionary in Worcester, where a large choir and orchestra were thought necessary for eighteenth-century works. I brought in a fine team of soloists – Sheila McShee and Arthur Reckless from London and Llechid Williams and Peter Salmon of Worcester Cathedral. Peter Salmon was a very fine young countertenor and a great success; for many of the packed audience it was the first experience of hearing a countertenor in the flesh. The hit of the performance was Sheila McShee, who sang like an angel and so impressed everyone, especially David Willcocks, that she was soon to be booked for a Three Choirs Festival. We went on to specialise in Handel oratorios, performing such works as *Jephtha* and *Samson*.

I met Barbara, my future wife, at my first introduction to the St John's Choral Society by Llechid Williams. Barbara was one of the sopranos, a keen singer and a very pretty girl and it is almost right to say it was love at first sight, but it is perhaps more correct to say that she ran away from me scared stiff when Llechid introduced us, so I must have been a frightening sight. We were married in Worcester Cathedral in 1956, waiting until 2 August when I was free from the choir and the school. This meant that the cathedral choir were not available to sing, but I gathered a few of the men together and some of the Singers came down from London and with Edgar Day playing the organ we had a memorable wedding in a grand setting.

For some time I had been a member of the BBC Midland Singers, whose recitals and concerts were broadcast from the Broad Street studios in Birmingham. On the evening of our wedding I had to broadcast the ballad opera *Hugh the Drover* by Ralph Vaughan Williams in the series 'Stories from the Operas'. There was me, having dashed up to Birmingham from Worcester, with confetti still in my hair and running down my legs, while singing away merrily. The fee was £4, just enough to pay for the honeymoon night at the Midland Hotel, and I will never forget the broadcast, which was made memorable for me by hearing James Johnston sing the role of Hugh. His lyrical Irish voice singing the wonderful Hugh's 'Song of the Road' rings in my ears to this day. The conductor was Leo Wurmser, who gave me some conducting lessons but did not seem to get on very well with his orchestras.

The day after the wedding and the broadcast we drove off to Wales in my little old Morris 8, a great character of a car that we called Lana. All old bangers had names then and when anyone asked why we called it Lana we said, 'Well, Lana Morris' (she was a British actress), or, 'Lana Turner' (an American film actress), 'as you have to turn the starting handle to get her going.' We liked dreadful jokes and puns and called our cat Magnificat, or Niffy for short. We spent our honeymoon in St David's, the incredible cathedral city on the west coast of Pembrokeshire. Harold Rattle had told me of the glories of this tiny city of just village size, with a glorious cathedral and a spectacular coastline. It was the tercentenary of the death of Thomas Tomkins, who was born in St David's, the son of the organist, and became organist of Worcester Cathedral, a post he held for fifty years. I was engaged to sing a number of concerts in St David's and, among the special events, a new organ case was opened by Harry Gabb, assistant organist of St Paul's. The rather small fees earned helped to pay for the honeymoon and we stayed in a cottage in Goat Street and had a wonderful time.

Returning to Worcester I continued my musical life trying to earn enough for two. Barbara continued her clerical job with the Inland Revenue and I took whatever musical engagements came my way, plus the cathedral and school. I sang a lot with the BBC Midland Singers under the chief conductor, John Lawe; I also did some private singing teaching and sang the solos in many concerts, some obtained by myself and others obtained by agents. The latter provided some of the most interesting, including *The Messiah* at Leyton, Bach cantatas in Birmingham Cathedral and Leamington Spa, Brahms's Requiem in Malvern and Hereford Cathedral, Matthew Passions in Tewkesbury, Oundle and Stamford, Bach's Christmas Oratorio in Ripon Cathedral and my favourite work, Haydn's *Creation*, in Bromyard, Leominster and Hornsey Town Hall with Highgate School choir.

There was an extra mouth to feed when Barbara produced our first son, David, in 1957 in Ronkswood Hospital. I did not want to pace the hospital waiting-room (in those days you were not encouraged to attend the births of your children – nowadays it is compulsory) and I had become very interested in archaeological discoveries, following Birmingham University's dig on the far side of the Old Palace from our flat, where they hoped to find the old Roman town of Worcester. I did my own excavation in my garden and found it very fascinating, producing pottery and coins going back to the Roman period. The most important discoveries included a silver stater of the pre-Roman Dubonii tribe, a very large, though smashed, Roman storage jar and a body, which worried Barbara when she returned from hospital with David. We decided that I should report the finding of the body to the police, so Barbara cleaned up the skull, which became detached from the rest of the body, put it in a shoe box from her father's shop (he sold and repaired shoes) and I took it to the local police station.

A large policewoman came to the counter and said, in a rather deep baritone, 'What do you want?' rather bossily.

'I've come to report finding a body,' I said, quite politely.

'What sort of body?' she said sneeringly.

'A human body,' I said. 'I've got his head in this box,' opening it and giving her a peep. She stepped back and went white, calling out for the sergeant. The sergeant called for the inspector and it became like 'Sam, pick up tha musket', where the battle cannot start until Sam picks up his musket and he won't do that until they work up to the Duke of Wellington himself. I didn't get to the Duke but I did get pretty high up the Worcester City police force and we had to hold a simple inquest in the garden, where I was able to show that I had not done the dirty deed.

The large jar got me interested in pottery as, after Barbara's mother and I had put all the bits together, it was found to have been repaired in Roman days with lead rivets. I suppose it was that pot which turned me into a potaholic and I began to watch the many Worcester sites that were being bulldozed, dug out and redeveloped. The papers called it the Rape of Worcester and a lot of fine buildings went in the name of progress, including the Lichgate and the original porcelain factory buildings, founded in 1751 but by that time being used as Dent's gloving factory.

A major change happened at the cathedral. David Willcocks left to become organist of King's College, Cambridge, and as a bit of a lark I ran a book on who would be appointed in his stead. No one bet on Douglas Guest, who followed Willcocks to Salisbury and then to Worcester, so I did well and ran a book on all subsequent appointments in major English cathedrals. Douglas Guest, who has only just died, was very different from Willcocks. He was tall, stately, quiet and rather shy but firm. Fairly quickly, a number of services were axed, especially the week-day mattins and litany, although the morning rehearsals were kept. I was rather sorry, as this meant losing some of the marvellous morning psalms, but it was a pointer to the future, many years later, when the psalms for the day were dropped from evensong. As I loved the psalms, this was a great blow to me.

The success of my book on the cathedral organists stakes led the choir to enter the football pools in the hope of making a big win, when we intended to buy our own cathedral and run it ourselves, without benefit of clergy. I used to check the results during the first lesson at Saturday's evensong, and our best result was a second prize, when we shared £170, but hope sprang eternal. They were a very sporting lot and when there was a test match, or an important game, on the country cricket grounds we had one of the vergers put the scores up on the nave pillar hymn-board, which could be seen from the quire stalls – there would be something like 326 (the total) then 6 (the wickets) and 28 for last man. I struck up close friendships with the vergers, who would let me take friends and visitors into rather special parts of the cathedral. One thing I would always show them was the tomb of the wicked King John. The king had asked to be buried between the tombs of the Worcester saints Oswald and Wulstan, to enlist their aid in getting to heaven. As an additional insurance, he left instructions that he should be mummified, dressed in monk's clothing with a cowl pulled down over his head and sandals on his feet, so that he could shuffle past St Peter unawares. Whether he got to heaven or not perhaps we will know one day.

In 1846 his tomb was opened and his body was found dressed as he had directed. They put bits of the king in a cabinet of curiosities on view to the public and the most gruesome piece was a thumb, encased in silver. One of the vergers used to ask me for any small bits of pottery, coins etc. which I found in excavations – very interesting for his son's school museum. Then he started asking for small bits of bodies, which are all over the place in an ancient town. I later found out what he was doing with them. He would see an American looking at King John's tomb, start chatting and drop the news that he had one of the King's fingers. He would sell a finger for £1 and a toe for £2 – he said toes were rarer – and must have done quite well. He was finally caught out; he had just sold a finger to an American for a pound and the purchaser looked down at the verger's feet where he had a bag of potatoes, intended for his lunch.

'Are they King John's?'

'No, King Edwards.'

'I'll buy them,' said the American.

I missed that verger a lot.

I passed the exam of the Fellowship of the London College of Music, which entitled me to a hood and gown and a slightly higher rate of pay at school. Barbara became pregnant again and in 1959 we had twin boys – John and Peter. This was a surprise, as we did not know it was going to be twins until a couple of days before the birth. (I, of course, did another excavation.) This obviously was going to put a big strain on finances and I needed a full-time secure job instead of the part-time schoolmastering. So I got a job as an inspector with the Gresham Life Assurance Company, whose branch was in Birmingham. This provided a decent car, which was useful, and although I was not a huge success in selling life insurance I did well enough to provide the boys with some pre-school education, see them into a nice primary school which had a good reputation and get Barbara and them a modern semi-detached house, which was more convenient than the Old Lodge Flat. I was able to keep the cathedral post as well, as the insurance company hours could be fairly flexible and some of it at night, but at times it became difficult to do both things.

The cathedral organist's post changed yet again. Douglas Guest took the post of organist of West-minster Abbey, shortly after Edgar Day had retired as assistant organist, and his place taken by Christopher Robinson. Naturally I ran a book on the new Worcester appointment, and with a bit of guidance from Daddy Dowse, who said that the Dean and Chapter had never been known to promote an assistant but always brought in an organist from outside, I made Christopher Robinson quite a high price. Only one person bet on him – Malcolm Darling – so I broke even. Christopher was a young man and like all the young organists coming into cathedrals at the time had new and youthful ideas. They all wanted to ease the older lay clerks out and replace them with younger singers, making the choirs famous on the national and international scene through gramophone records, public recitals and overseas tours. None of this had been done by previous organists; I think the only time we had left the cathedral (apart from going to Hereford and Gloucester for the Three Choirs Festivals) was for a funeral service for Lady Coventry in Croome Park, the wedding of Llechid Williams' son at Bourton on the Water and the reconsecration of Coventry Cathedral. (The Worcester choir was invited to join in this as Coventry had originally been carved out of Worcester diocese. Our hardened old pros did not enjoy it as there was an obnoxious precentor who ranted and raved and we were given a packed lunch of a couple of sandwiches and an apple. Daddy Dowse had an apoplectic fit.)

The choir changed, happily in a friendly way. Even though the oldest departed, it was done kindly. I had been on the committee of management of the Choir Benevolent Fund for a number of years. They provide financial help to sick and infirm singers of cathedral choirs (I still serve on the committee), and they began to hear some rather terrible stories. One new organist called his choir together and said in a very cheerful voice, 'Anyone who has been here more than ten years had better start looking for another job.' That was very symptomatic of the wind of change that was blowing through cathedrals. This was not only in

England. I was having lunch with my hosts in a United States city and a fellow guest was the recently appointed organist of the local cathedral. He proudly announced that he had just got rid of a singer who had been in the choir for *twenty years!* When I said that I had been a lay clerk in Worcester for longer than that he shut up, to the pleasure of my host. There is not now the continuity that there used to be of lay clerks going into a choir when they were young men and being carried out in a box.

The Worcester choir began to make a number of gramophone recordings under Christopher Robinson and his assistant organist Harry Bramma. A particularly fine record was of anthems by Edward Elgar, in which two of my sons, David and Peter, took part. They had joined as choristers, having developed fine singing voices through Barbara singing to them when they were young, and received a marvellous musical training as well as a splendid education at the King's School. Our other son, John, had no singing voice, so did not become a chorister but passed his eleven plus from Red Hill primary school and went to the King's School by that avenue. Although he missed out on a musical training, he developed an interest in fossils and ceramics from an early age, so helped me on excavations.

The cathedral choir did a number of continental tours, to Germany and France, once singing a service in Notre Dame in Paris. It was a great period for the development of musicians among the choristers, the

Cleobury brothers becoming especially famous – Stephen as organist of King's College, Cambridge, and conductor of the BBC Singers, and Nicholas as a freelance conductor. Another famous pair of brothers were the Darlingtons. During this period I was a Special Constable in the local force, mainly getting called out to appear at elections to guard the polling booth and on special occasions, such as when the lowly Worcester City football team played mighty Liverpool in the FA Cup. I was on duty for the match, so would have seen it for nothing but the game was called off at the last minute owing to the condition of the pitch, and many of the visiting Liverpool fans gave away their tickets in disgust as they could not return to Worcester the next Wednesday. So, I was there when David beat Goliath with a goal by Roy Paul, the Worcester captain and rather long retired English player. Worcester City have never reached such heights again.

Although I was a Special long enough to get my long-service medal (fifteen years of undetected crime), I must admit that I did not go out on duty very much. My main task was to conduct the Worcester City police male voice choir, which was founded by the Chief Constable, Eric Abbott, who had run a similar choir in Leeds. It was not only a good thing for morale but as the concerts were charity events in places like village halls it was also thought to be very good public relations. The choir was a mixture of regulars and Specials, and although not

large we had a great spirit and all enjoyed themselves. Our greatest moment was when we competed
in the Hereford music festival male voice choir
competition against a fine Welsh choir, who not only
sang beautifully but also looked smart in matching
ties and blazers. My rag tag and bobtail group were
scared stiff at such competition but I told them to
relax and enjoy themselves and to remember
Worcester City against Liverpool. We sang 'Comrades
in Arms' and 'Yellow Bird' and the adjudicator must
have been taken by little David against Goliath,
because she gave us the cup. I think the Welsh choir
were a bit peeved and there was a punch-up in the
car park afterwards. After I retired from the force the
choir merged with the Hereford police choir and still
give concerts. I have recently had the pleasure of
compèring some of these concerts, in Hereford
Cathedral and Symphony Hall, Birmingham, and
they even let me conduct the choir and band.

I remember one day when I did a duty, when the
regulars were to have their photograph taken at the
station and the Specials were called out to run the
City. I was put on duty at The Cross, the main
crossroad in the centre of the city, and it gave a great
sense of power to hold up one line of cars, bring the
others on with a wave of my hand, like conducting
an orchestra. But things began to go wrong, the lines
of traffic did not obey and before I knew what was
happening there were four lines of cars nose to nose
with me in the middle. I slipped through the cars and

went off to have a cup of tea in a café in New Street,
When I returned, all the traffic had gone – how they
did it I don't know.

My St John's Choral Society had to finish when
Worcester City Council turned the Public Hall into a
skating rink, prior to pulling it down during the
'Rape of Worcester', thus depriving us of this
splendid concert hall. We went out in blaze with a
performance of *Samson* in which David Johnston sang
the title role. Our last concert was an April Fool's Day
event when we had a dig at the Council by performing the Skater's Waltz for solo skater and
orchestra. There was a wonderful new work by Peter
Beresford-Jones, an ex-Cathedral chorister, who set
the poem 'Black-Eyed Susan' for a narrator, per-
cussion orchestra and wordless choir. It was billed as
'the first *and last* performance', and at the end the
composer tore up his manuscript so that it could not
be performed again.

I conducted some shows for the Malvern Operatic
Society, having played in the orchestra for them
earlier. The principal was Professoressa Maria Lloyd-
Foulkes, a fiery and exciting Italian-born teacher, and
it was said that conductors only lasted three shows.
That was true. I conducted *The Merry Widow* by Franz
Lehár, which went very well and was their first show
that made a profit. I got on very well with Maria and
her soloists and chorus and got my own little band
together. The lovely theatre made a splendid and
inspiring venue, as it had mounted first perfor-

mances of Shaw's plays during the pre-war Malvern Festivals. I was told that Errol Flynn had first trod the professional boards there. There was a wonderful mood with a good band, well drilled orchestra and dancers and fine principals. I enjoyed myself enormously, swinging through the waltzes and the can-can with spirit. Another Lehár followed the next year and for my third (and last) show they decided on something more daring and they produced *West Side Story*. What a difficult work that was to bring off, but what a splendid score! Maria's two daughters played the Puerto Rican parts with Latin fire and I tried to get an orchestra more used to playing Beethoven to let their hair down and play the tricky jazz parts. I had a hard enough job just beating time, each bar varying from 5/8 to 7/8 or something worse, but we struggled through and by the last night were doing pretty well. It was a shame when the week came to an end and I can never listen to such numbers as 'America' or 'Maria' without remembering it.

I had been watching out in the local papers for a job that I would find more sympathetic than the insurance business and towards the end of 1966 there was an advert for the post of curator of the Dyson Perrins Museum and the Worcester Royal Porcelain Company. I had developed an interest in Worcester porcelain and with my archaeological ceramic discoveries and enthusiasm for pottery-making under Geoffrey Whiting I applied for the post. I had an interview with the directors of Royal Worcester and the Trustees of the museum. The chairman was a grand old chap named Joseph Grimson. I was asked if I would be happy to direct the public tours of the factory as well as running the museum and of course I agreed. They were interested in my archaeological interests, especially when I suggested that a lot of knowledge about the history of the company might come from the ground, and they were not unhappy with my continuing in the cathedral choir.

A week later, I was told that I had the post. I resigned from the Gresham Life Assurance and became curator of Royal Worcester, little thinking that this second major changing of horses in mid-stream was going to lead to the most important part of my life and work.

5

Royal Worcester

The history of porcelain-making in Worcester went back to 1751, when Dr John Wall and fourteen partners formed a company, though they took over an earlier factory which went bankrupt in Bristol, which had been formed by potters who had a factory in Limehouse in London, which failed about 1747. The history was long and complicated, with different factories in Worcester which merged at different times, and I was helped to understand this by the previous curator, a lovely man named Cyril Shingler who had come to Worcester from the Potteries to work in the pattern room. He became the curator in 1951 when the Dyson Perrins Museum was opened to the public by Princess Elizabeth, to celebrate the bicentenary of the founding of the company. The collection of Worcester porcelain, formed and given to the Trust by Dyson Perrins, was the finest in the world, but to display it properly large premises were needed rather than the old Regency showroom. The Trustees were able to purchase the Victorian St Peter's Church of England school (in which my wife was educated) and the first task was to move the collection into the new building when it was ready and fitted with some of the old and some new cases in two large galleries. This was a major undertaking and Cyril Shingler stayed on for six months to help in this. I certainly learned a lot about Worcester porcelain very quickly by being able to handle so many fine and interesting pieces as we moved the precious and fragile objects from the old building to the new in large factory ware baskets and arranged them in their new home.

I had worked out a historical sequence. The works of the Doctor Wall period and the successors Flight and Barr, which were made in the factory on the far side of the cathedral and Old Palace, were put in the one gallery which had lovely daylight. The wares of Chamberlain's factory and the Worcester Royal Porcelain Company, produced on the site where the company is still, were put in the other. So the one gallery had the beautiful and subtle wares of the eighteenth and early nineteenth centuries and the other the wares of the nineteenth and twentieth centuries, including those of the high Victorian period and the huge Chicago Exhibition vase, culminating in the spectacular birds modelled by Dorothy Doughty. When the new museum was opened by the Lord Lieutenant of Worcestershire, Viscount Cobham, in June 1967 it was with a great sense of pride that I surveyed my handiwork and the museum remained basically the same for the seventeen years that I was curator.

I had to answer the many questions and queries

posed by visitors and correspondents and did a quick crash course building up a mass of information on the history, wares made and craftsmen involved. I also had to direct and organise the tours of the factory and while there were not so many visitors in the winter months, they quickly built up through the spring and summer to a total of many thousands a year. I had a head guide and a dozen guides to take the parties of up to ten visitors at a time on an hour's tour of the factory, for which the visitors paid about a pound. I had to make sure these ran smoothly and train new guides. It was also one of my jobs to take any VIPs round the factory myself, and to that end the Trustees wanted me to learn the ins and outs of the factory and the production as soon as possible.

I had a wonderful couple of weeks going into every department of the factory, learning from the foremen the inner secrets of the processes. The skills were mindbending and I spent hours in the company of some of the greatest craftsmen in the world, who were very generous with their time and knowledge, though they told me that a few years earlier few would have done this. I was told of the painting family, the Stintons, who if anyone came into their room would down their brushes, fold their arms and refuse to paint until the interloper left the room. George Owen, who did the most miraculous reticulating (piercing of the clay while it was wet), would never let *anyone* into his room, working behind a locked door for fear that someone would learn his secrets. But I had great kindness from them all and they even patiently tried to teach me to do these crafts, though with little success.

I will never forget them. The foreman engraver, Percy Burgess, had arms the size of tree trunks but could engrave the most delicate designs onto thin sheets of copper for printing patterns onto porcelain; Percy Lewis, master gilder, was then in his eighties, but could do the most incredible perfect gilding until his eyesight went; Ivor Williams did ornamental and raised gilding with jewelling and had a piece in the Ashmolean Museum; the girl flowermakers could produce the most lifelike flowers out of a lump of clay body – when I tried it the clay just broke and crumbled; foreman caster Bob Bradley showed me how the many small parts were first cast in liquid slip and then stuck together to form complete birds, horses or human figures; Terry Lewis passed on many of the lessons, learned from Bob Bradley, that enabled him to produce a hundred figures in a week, all fit to be passed by his master; the complicated process of making the plaster moulds was shown to me by George Morris.

But the greatest joy and honour was in meeting Harry Davis, the painter whose work I had admired for years. There I was, in Harry's little room at the top of a spiral stepped turret, watching him paint a masterpiece on a plaque, a copy of a Corot scene. He was as frightened of meeting me as I was of meeting him.

'What will your next painting be, Mr Davis?' I asked.

He rummaged in a cupboard among bits of paper and card and I held my breath as I thought that I was going to see the original sketch-books. When he emerged with a chocolate box cover showing a hunting scene, saying, 'Wouldn't that make a great plaque?' my heart sank. My idol had feet of clay. The painters were all taught to do fine copying in the most difficult medium of ceramic colours, and I determined there and then that I must write a book about their lives and work, telling the public how they learned their craft, letting these basically very shy, hidden craftsmen come to life in print.

This quick indoctrination was important for when I started getting requests from the company to show VIPs around. These ranged from stars of 'stage, screen and radio', as we used to say in the days before TV, to sporting heroes, titled people and even royals. Royal Worcester had a great name worldwide, and I showed the visitors with pride the Royal Warrants dating from King George III in 1789 and from all subsequent monarchs, the examples of royal services in the Museum and pattern room, and especially the skills of the present-day craftsmen. There were many VIPs, but some of those who made a big impression on me and the workers on the factory floor included Stephane Grappelli, the fabulous jazz violinist, who was playing at Malvern, and Stan Mellor, the steeple-chase jockey, who was presented with a Royal

Worcester model of a horse to celebrate winning a thousand races. Stan was asked by the men painters if he had a good horse for the afternoon race meeting at Worcester; he called for a newspaper and pointed to a little-fancied horse, The Leap. Everyone dashed to the bookies' at lunchtime and the horse led from start to finish, romping home at 14 to 1.

In the days when the visiting cricket tourists played their first match at Worcester, the whole team would tour the factory and sign their names, and a plate with their signatures would be produced in time for them to take one home, with a few more made for sale. So I took round all the great teams from 1967 and found that many cricketers really enjoyed porcelain. We had frequent visits from famous England players such as John Edrich, Don Kenyon and Basil D'Oliviera, and just before I left the Museum I did an interview with Brian Johnston on *Down Your Way* in which we talked about these great cricketers. We talked about Sir Donald Bradman who wrote to me a number of times about his most prized possession – a superb covered vase painted by Harry Davis with a scene of Don playing on the Worcester cricket ground with the cathedral in the background, given to the great man in 1938 for scoring a double century each time he played against the poor county on his first three tours – 1930, 1934 and 1938. Sir Donald has now given this wonderful pot to his Museum.

The most amusing sporting visit must be that of the Newcastle United football team in 1972. They were staying at the Giffard Hotel in Worcester while waiting to replay Hereford United in the Cup. In the first match at Newcastle, the Hereford minnows had held Newcastle to a hard-fought two-all draw, and the mighty Newcastle must have been fed up at having to go through it all again against such lowly opposition, especially when the replay was twice postponed because of the weather. To give the Newcastle players something to keep their minds off the wait they were invited to tour the factory, so I came to conduct some of the most famous players in the football league, such heroes as Malcolm Macdonald, McFaul the Irish goalkeeper, Frank Clark the left back and Bobby Moncur the Scottish captain. I'm afraid that the potters gave them a bit of a tough time, telling the 'Magpies' that Hereford would murder them, reminding them what Worcester City had done to Liverpool. No one really believed it, of course – surely Newcastle would stroll through the game and enter the next round. As it turned out, it was one of the biggest upsets in football history. Although Malcolm Macdonald (Supermac) scored for Newcastle, Hereford won 2-1 through goals by Ricky George and Ronnie Radford, including *the* great goal, a shot from the halfway line that McFaul never even saw. This goal is shown so frequently on TV that Newcastle United supporters must hate Hereford.

Among non-sporting VIPs that I conducted around the factory were Princess Alexandra, Edward Heath, Margaret Thatcher and President Reagan's son and grandson. Royal and political visits impose big problems. The police carry out inspections and usually there are bodyguards, so everything is a bit tense. It is a lot more relaxed when actors such as Donald Sinden come. He was playing Shakespeare's *Henry VIII* at Stratford and the local paper had him looking at the Royal Worcester model of the King. The most important visit was by the Queen and the Duke of Edinburgh when she was to distribute the Royal Maundy money at Worcester Cathedral in 1980. We put on an exhibition of royal services and figures made by Royal Worcester in the Commandery, across the road from the factory. Its design was by Peter Ewence, chief designer of the factory. I had the honour of showing the royal couple around, together with the chairman of the company, Lyn Davies.

After the Perrins Museum was opened, I was able to devote some time to archaeological work. I was still helping to watch building site excavations in Worcester, especially on the massive Lich Street site, and bottomed a deep medieval well, finding a magnificent large three-handled jug that had been imported from Santoinge les Pots in France somewhere around AD 1250. This was in 160 pieces and was wonderfully put together by the British Museum and is now a prized item in Worcester City Museum. I isolated and cleared parts of medieval middens (cesspits) which were full of fascinating things preserved in the black sludge – seeds, insects, leaves, even leather shoes. The shoes were fascinating, as they were of the type which had turned-up ends, like the winkle-picker shoes that were all the rage at the time I was finding them. This surprised all the site workers, who couldn't believe that those I was finding were as old as I said they were. I got on very well with the navvies, who were great chaps, and I would get phone calls at the Museum if they saw something that they thought might be interesting. I got called across to see a complete Roman blackware pot, found beneath what turned out to be the bank of the Roman ditch around the Roman city. I took it back to the Museum and cleaned it in the sink and was surprised when it seemed to be full of the remains of a rabbit stew. This was sent to Birmingham University to be analysed and the information came back that the bones were those of a newborn human baby. I was told by Philip Barker, who had arrived to take over responsibility for the archaeological work in Worcester, that the baby had probably been buried deliberately under the bank for good luck. And I had washed it up in the sink!

One old ceramic factory site in Worcester that I became interested in was Graingers, which started about 1806 and finished in 1902, having been bought up by Royal Worcester in 1889. Many of the old buildings still stood and some were owned by the firm of Heenan and Froude, who kindly gave me permission to follow a deep pipe line across the site. This went through one of the old kilns and Peter Ewence (who, as well as being the factory designer, produced drawings for the Ministry of Works) drew a plan of this and I managed to gather a mass of wasters – bits of porcelain thrown away during making or after firing. These proved of great interest to Geoffrey Godden, the ceramic historian, and Dr Bernard Watney, later President of the English Ceramic Circle, and they encouraged me to do a major excavation of the original site of Worcester Porcelain. After the buildings had been demolished during the late 1950s and a large technical college built on part of the site, the rest of it lay as a rough car park, owned by the Corporation of Worcester. I got permission from them to carry out an excavation – it helped that the Mayor and Town Clerk for the time being were ex officio Trustees of the Perrins Museum.

I laid out a twenty-yard-long trench running up the site from the River Severn side, and set to work. First came the grind of taking off the top five feet or so of hard compacted rubble, helped by some interested friends from the factory, especially Peter Ewence and Neal French, designers, and David Peplow, a painter. Below this we began to find our first wasters from the original factory: at first bits of floor tiles from the 1850s tile works; then a quantity of eighteenth-century teapot covers all smashed up in a level, which we decided were early Dr Wall period covers kept at the factory for some fifty years in case of need, then smashed up so that no one could use them, and dumped. As we progressed deeper and deeper it was vitally necessary to keep all the wasters found in one level separate from those in other levels: the deeper down we got, the earlier the date of the pieces, unless a rubbish pit had been cut through earlier levels, in which case the pit had to be cleared first before going on. It became harder and harder to get the spoil of clay, soil, ash and bits of kiln furniture out and I found David Peplow's adaptation of an ancient Egyptian water-raising system of great help. But it remained to raise the spoil by bucket and rope when we got down to the fifteen- and twenty-foot mark.

My son John by this time had become extremely interested and knowledgeable about porcelain and he played a great part, especially in sorting out the wasters, which Barbara had washed up in the kitchen sink. The benefit of finding unfinished wasters on an actual factory site is that you know for a certainty that they were made there and nowhere else. It was not possible to rely on the finding of glazed and finished pieces, which could have come from any-where, and we found many examples of Chinese porcelain and Staffordshire earthenware that had obviously been on the factory for use or study. Geoffrey Godden had asked me to look out for a particular type of porcelain, carrying what was called a 'disguised numeral' mark underneath transfer-printed pieces of a bright blue colour, having a translucence of a straw colour when held up to the light. This range of ware of about 1780-90 was always held to be from the Caughley factory in Shropshire although Geoffrey Godden had not found any examples at Caughley when he examined thousands of wasters when that site was dug up by bulldozers. He strongly suspected that the type was Worcester, which flew in the face of considered opinion, and his joy was unconfined when I began finding them in the 1780s levels.

If these wares had to change from Caughley to Worcester, there would be great consternation in ceramic circles. Caughley was not thought to be as good as Worcester and the text books of previous experts and authors often ascribed to their favourite factories the finest pieces and to other factories the not-so-good. Would the public believe my new findings? I thought I would try it out on a hard-bitten old Worcester porcelain antique dealer, Mr Philpott. I got on quite well with him, though he could be a bit prickly with many people. He hated selling anything – the pieces were his own babies – and no one was allowed to buy more than one piece. He hated American collectors and would order them out of his shop. Apparently one had had the temerity to offer to buy his whole stock! His method of deciding if a piece was Worcester was the classic one – he had a bare 100-watt light-bulb and would put this inside the pot. If it glowed a lovely green colour it must be Worcester. When I showed him the wasters from the 1780s levels, with a translucence of a strawy orange and explained that they had come from the factory site so must be Worcester, I expected to be chucked out of the shop, but he gave a deep chuckle and announced, 'We've been wrong all along!' The poor chap died soon after that (but not, I hope, from the shock); but I had my proof and both Geoffrey Godden and I announced the great discovery – Geoffrey in a book entitled *Caughley and Worcester Porcelain* and I in *Worcester Porcelain 1751-1793*.

There were yet more surprises in deeper levels. Among these were the finds of very early pieces of 1751 or so, right from the early years of the factory. The fascinating thing about many of these pieces was that they were exactly like the porcelain always called Lund's Bristol, a very rare and valuable class. I had to tell everyone that much of what was called Lund's Bristol was, in fact, Worcester and coined a new title for the early wares, which might be Bristol but could just as easily be early Worcester – I called the class Bristol/Worcester. Many collectors would not accept these changes easily and it took a whole series of excavations in the years that followed, when we concentrated on the earliest levels, to confirm these facts. In these later excavations son John played a very full part, as also did Dr Malcolm Nixon, a ceramic historian. The most important single piece that we found in the first dig was a model of part of a rare figure called *Cupid at Vulcan's Forge*. Geoffrey Godden found an illustration of this in a book about the wares of the Longton Hall factory by Dr Bernard Watney, who owned the figure. He kindly sold it to the Museum and I put it on display when we opened a special exhibition of the results of the excavation. The exhibition, opened by James Kiddell of Sotheby's, who was Chairman of the English Ceramic Circle, was an enormous success, comparing the wasters with finished pieces, proving for the first time that they were of undoubted Worcester origin.

As well as working on the excavations and at the museum, factory and cathedral, I did a number of lecture series for the extra-mural department of Birmingham University. These were either music lectures, when David and Peter would come and help, or ceramic ones, when John would come with me. Sometimes all three sons came, as they did to one of the villages – Great Witley in Worcestershire. One of the twenty evenings I was due to go, I had a call at the factory from No. 10 Downing Street. Would I go and see the Prime Minister, Edward Heath? I arranged for someone from the extra-mural group to fetch the three boys, to run the lesson until I got there, and went to London. This was my first visit to No. 10 Downing Street, and I found another person waiting to see Mr Heath, a Victoria and Albert Museum specialist on early Chinese porcelain. We chatted until we got the call into the inner sanctum. Mr Heath was in a jovial but careful mood. The Chinese expert was shown some early celadon that Mr Heath wanted authenticated, which was done. Then the Prime Minister showed me some porcelain plates that he had bought at a fair as Worcester. Were they genuine and good buys? I was able to confirm that they were indeed genuine, dated about 1815, but pointed out that several pieces had been restored and were probably not good buys. I think he must have appreciated this honesty because we struck up a friendship which has lasted for twenty-five years. He came to Worcester a number of times, particularly to see the Museum collection, and took a great interest in Worcester porcelain. He invited Barbara and me to visit his flat in Downing Street and we saw the private side of the man – cultivated, artistic and rather vulnerable.

On one occasion I took Mr Heath to see a wonderful collection of ceramics in Rous Leach Court near Evesham in Worcestershire. This wonderful Elizabethan mansion was the home of Thomas Burn, one of the world's great collectors – of early English oak furniture, delft and slipware pottery, which looked magnificent in an early setting. The long gallery contained a fantastic collection of eighteenth- century English porcelain, mainly Worcester, Chelsea, Bow and Longton Hall. Some of these pieces were put out on two fine early harpsichords, on which Edward Heath greatly enjoyed playing Bach. Barbara and I had become great friends with Tom Burn and he took to our family, especially John. I think he would have liked John to become curator of the collection, when it was intended to leave it to the town of Evesham. Mr Burn allowed me to bring special visitors over and take them around the collection. He also let John do this and one day John, only eleven years of age, conducted a party of leading auctioneers around the museum, factory and Rous Lench Court and in the party was Christopher Weston, the head of Phillips. He was so impressed with John that, four years later, he invited him to take a position in the ceramics department and now he has risen to be a director of the firm.

Rous Lench Court was an extraordinary place, not just for its great collections but also for its eccentric owner. A master bespoke tailor, he put all the money he made out of tailoring into buying antiques. I once had a suit made by his firm. Tom took the measurements and James Newman, his servant, took them down. I was let into some of the terms of the trade – Tom kept on mentioning 'AIF'.

'What does that mean, Mr Tom?'

'It means "All In Front", an indication of your shape to the cutter.'

I had several fittings at the Court and while the material was lovely, the suit never fitted.

'It will work up,' or, 'It'll be all right when you've worn it a couple of times' – a bit like Grace Brothers' store in *Are You Being Served?* But it never did.

The relationship between master and servant was very strange. I used to warn visitors in advance not to worry too much when they started to swear at each other or if James hit Mr Tom with a frying-pan. James would be given the sack during each visit but would counter by saying that he couldn't be sacked as he hadn't had a holiday for six years, or been paid for six months. This would be put on like a theatrical act to get everyone worked up until Mr Tom would say, 'Bring out the bottles, James,' and peace would be restored. The place was very cold in the winter – there was only one fire, in the main drawing-room, in a grand fireplace rescued from William Randolph Hearst's warehouse; Mr Tom had brought it back from America in a stateroom on the *Queen Mary*. He slept in a cold bedroom, warmed by a few glasses of whiskey and his two poodles sleeping with him. The poodles ran the place and when Barbara bought a poodle from the Rous Lench breeder, the three poodles had poodle parties in the Court. They could do no wrong and if they left 'little messages' or cocked their legs on the beams or furniture, Tom would beam like mad and say, 'Don't worry, it's good for the oak.' He smoked like mad and the smoky wood fire added to the fun, causing all the slipware and delft in the main room to be coloured a deep mahogany. When a special party was coming, we would go over and wash these wonderful pieces in bowls of water. What joy it was to see the true colours emerge, or a date appear! I always told the visitors to watch out for the poodles eating from a dated delft bowl. We learned such a lot from being able to handle these fine pieces.

I took quite a few Americans to Rous Lench Court and also showed them around the Museum and factory. One big party was the Wedgwood International Seminar, several hundreds of them, and my sons got time off from school to help. The success of this led me to think of starting a Friends of the Dyson Perrins Museum in the hope that this would develop a body of people that would help support the Museum and spread the gospel of Worcester porcelain around the world. This made a good start at a meeting chaired by the Mayor of Worcester, Mrs Joyce Brown; Jack Collins became the secretary and numbers increased over the years. Like the excavations it was done without a lot of money. My wife and family were the mainspring, plus Jack Collins and the next secretary, Malcolm Nixon, and a hard-working committee. We put on visits to great collections, lectures and parties in the Museum and bulletins to keep overseas members in touch.

With this growing interest from America, a very important market for Royal Worcester, the Managing Director, Robert Steven, had me do my first lecture tour of the United States. I had the help of Dewey Lee Curtis, curator of Pennsbury Manor near Philadelphia, in organising this. He had brought a party of keen ceramic collectors to Worcester and he fixed up a wonderful first lecture tour for me, though it was very tiring. In that tour I flew over most of that vast country, lecturing in some of the world's great museums, such as the Metropolitan in New York, the Smithsonian in Philadelphia and the Art Institute in Chicago as well as many provincial museums, and did a number of TV and radio shows and dozens of newspaper interviews. The success of this led to an annual tour of America.

110

Returning to Worcester, I finished the major book *Royal Worcester Porcelain from 1862*, which covered the history in a very human way and dealt with the craftsmen and their lives. The book became very popular, going through a large number of printings, and I followed it with a book that filled up the middle years, covering the history and superb productions of the Flight and Barr period. I had two other books published; one, *British Pottery and Porcelain*, is still in print after twenty-five years, and in the other, *Coffee Pots and Teapots*, I expressed my love and admiration of these wonderful objects. I suppose I am a teapotaholic among many other things. Sons David and John were to help me in the production of a later book, *The Sandon Guide to Royal Worcester Figures, 1900-1970*, and John and I wrote the first and definitive book *Grainger Worcester Porcelain*. I missed John's help when he went to Phillips; then David went to work for Lloyd's Bank and Peter went off to Bristol to be an accountant. So the chicks had flown the nest.

The most important thing that happened at this period was that I met and got on very well with Arthur Negus. He was the son of a Reading antique dealer and moved to Gloucester to become sales clerk and cataloguer to the old county auctioneers Bruton Knowles. I saw him many times at auctions, sitting up on the rostrum, taking down the prices, putting in bids that had been left with him by absent bidders and coming over as a wonderfully warm, avuncular person. He knew Tom Burn of Rous Leach Court, who often attended auctions when there was some fine early oak or ceramics, and although Arthur's main knowledge and love was furniture we would often talk about pots. I was delighted when the BBC discovered him and put him into two early antiques programmes that they were doing from the Bristol studios. The first was *Collectors' World*, a kind of kaleidoscopic programme of bits and pieces. I had been involved with a wonderful film that *Collectors' World* had made about Dorothy Doughty and the superb models of American birds and flowers made by Royal Worcester for the American market, the only complete collection of which in this country was in the Dyson Perrins Museum.

I was asked to go to Bristol to do a *Collectors' World* item about teapots and I took some interesting ones with me. The presenter of the programme was Hugh Scully and he was so nice and friendly that I lost my nerves about my first appearance on TV. I had a lovely happy chat with Arthur Negus about teapots and the hit of the evening was my Cadogan teapot, named after Lady Cadogan, who had brought the strange wine-pot shape back from China to be made as a fun teapot by Rockingham and Spode. The peculiar thing about the Cadogan teapot is that it has no cover to take off to pour the boiling water in and Arthur said to me, 'How do you fill it? Down the spout?'

I explained that you turned it upside down and

filled it through the hole in the bottom with hot strained tea.

Arthur said, 'I don't believe you!' so I picked up a jug of water and poured the pretend strained tea into the hole.

Arthur said, 'What do you do next? Put a cork in the bottom?'

'No,' I said, 'you say a few magic words, pray like mad and turn it over.'

Arthur was amazed when the water did not pour back from the hole, and said, 'It's gone up your sleeve!' But I assured him that it hadn't and poured it out from the spout into a cup. Everyone was suitably impressed – none more than I, as I was not really sure it would work as well as it did. I still do not know how it works, even though a potter has made a new Cadogan with my modelled face on one side and son John's on the other, which is going to be made by my new ceramic company, Bronté Porcelain.

Arthur Negus made a great hit with the public, who loved the gentle burr in his voice and his lovely countryman personality. He was no spring chicken when he was discovered and BBC Bristol found the correct vehicle for him – *Going for a Song*. This was done at first in the Bristol studios (Bristol has made itself pre-eminent in programmes about antiques and wildlife) in front of a small invited audience, and was an artistic, educational game show. In the centre of a table sat Max Robertson, who was a famous tennis commentator with an interest in antiques. He had a box under his table into which you were not allowed to see beforehand. To his left sat two well known people from the world of films or TV, who saw the item first. They had to guess at what the item was and put a value on it; the one who was nearer to the actual price got a point and the one who had the most points at the end of the programme received a prize of an antique. At the other end of the table sat Arthur Negus and a guest specialist whose task it was to see the item next, say exactly what it was and write down the value on a piece of paper, which a girl would put up on a board for the viewers to see. The viewers had already been shown details of what the item was, so the experts were under great pressure to get it right.

We had a run through, with different items to the real ones, to make sure that everyone knew what was happening and to get the half-hour timing right. I remember on my first run-through, one of the items was a pair of Staffordshire figures of a shoe cobbler and his wife. I always like a bit of fun so I said they were made in Staffordshire about 1830, so they were a couple of Old Cobblers! Arthur was horrified and said, 'You mustn't say rude things like that on the BBC!' I was glad it wasn't the live programme.

My first *Going for a Song* went extremely well. The showbiz guests were a husband and wife team who were appearing in a BBC TV soap called *The Brothers* about a family lorry haulage business – Liza Goddard and Colin Baker (who later portrayed Dr Who). The first piece I had was a Caughley cider mug that I easily identified and valued at the going rate of £100. The next item was really for Arthur, a bone French prisoner-of-war model of a spinner by a spinning wheel. Arthur said he didn't know what it was. (He was rather good at doing that and the public loved it – he knows almost everything and yet he's honest when he doesn't know.)

'Yes, you do,' cooed Max Robertson, 'you've seen something like that before.'

'No, I haven't,' said Arthur, so Max asked me if I knew. Inspiration struck, or heaven must have been tuned in, because I said I wondered if it could be French prisoner-of-war.

'Well done,' said Max, and even Arthur was beaming. So I was in a euphoric state when the next item came out of the box, a five-inch-high bell figurine, made in Staffordshire in salt glaze, with manganese stripes and eyes. I knew it instantly, it came from Rous Lench Court and I had handled this little beauty many times. Should I say I knew it? Would that upset things and make the public think it was a put-up job? I didn't say that I had known it, but accurately described and dated it, putting a value of £1,500 on it, a pretty accurate price. It is a sobering thought that after Tom Burn's death, years later, when the collection had to be sold to pay death duties, I went to the auction hoping to buy it, but it went for £48,000, so it shows how values can change.

Later programmes went to great houses and used items in the house as the competition pieces. I did an enjoyable *Going for a Song* at the beautiful National Trust property Stourhead, and the programmes proved so popular that we were always being asked to participate in performances for charities or local churches. One was put on by the auctioneers Bruton Knowles in a Worcestershire village hall. As one of the items, son John made a pretend Worcester eighteenth-century Worcester basket, cut out the holes by hand and painted it in cobalt oxide. It really looked marvellous, and when Arthur Negus was asked to identify it he said the expected things – made in 1775, very fine and worth hundreds. I was then asked when it was made, and when I said, 'Half past six last Monday' the audience collapsed and Arthur took it like the great sport he was. The basket was auctioned in aid of the charity and fetched the price of an eighteenth-century one.

John was always especially interested in Worcester blue and white patterns, following the excavation discoveries, and I was always on at him to do a major book covering these fascinating patterns, with the help of Neal French, the Royal Worcester designer who had always had a fascination with them and did superb pen-and-ink drawings of them. The idea dragged on for years until we met Larry Branyan, an American lawyer who was working in England with an oil company. He had come to Worcester to accompany his wife, an enthusiast about early porcelain. She was attending a weekend seminar about blue and white Worcester porcelain put on by

RVS Enterprises, run by Judy Watts, for whom I had done a number of such things. Larry Branyan had no interest in porcelain when he came but fell in love with Worcester blue and white, was mesmerised watching David Peplow paint the patterns and won the prize for giving the best titles to the often humorous patterns. He bought a number of rare patterns, which you could do then, and had the qualities to push the other two into producing the book. The book put blue and white on the map, illustrating all the patterns with code numbers and names so that they could be more easily described in catalogues. We put on a fine exhibition in the Museum, which visitors entered through a huge willow-pattern type plate.

When I was writing the Flight and Barr book I wanted to see all the Worcester pieces in the royal collections, as so many had been made for the royal family. The Lord Chamberlain's office gave me permission to visit the porcelain collections in Buckingham Palace, Windsor Castle and Sandringham, and Barbara and I had a fabulous time drooling over these wonderful things. In the china pantry of Buckingham Palace, which seemed the length of Oxford Street, were arranged all the incredible royal services, ranging from Sèvres and Worcester to Minton, each service in its special cabinet, and we had the joy of seeing how a Worcester service was used, with the waiters taking the pieces upstairs and returning them afterwards, when the keeper of the pantry washed each piece up by hand in a plastic bowl (no washing-up machine) before it went back into its cabinet. We asked him how some of the rich services of the past were used at table. Some were strange harlequins, a curious mixture of landscapes, shells, flowers, feathers, birds. Did they just have one set of plates of the same pattern on the table – just the flowers, say? No, was the answer, they are mixed and matched. When we said that the table must look confusing, we were told that it was good for conversation: when talk dried up, you could always ask what was on you neighbour's plate. On our way home, it crossed our mind that when people came to dinner we would put out our harlequin service – a bit of Worcester, a bit of Wedgwood, a bit of Woolworths – and if the visitor looked surprised we would say, 'Well, it's what the Queen does!'

The royal visits were not only wonderful and helpful but they had an exciting development. I had been surprised to see no examples of a famous Worcester pattern, the 'Royal Lily'. This had been based upon a Chinese blue and white pattern and made at Worcester from the 1780s. (I was able to confirm this from the archaeological digs.) A service had been bought by King George III on his visit to Worcester in 1788 and the following year he granted the company his Royal Warrant. I was sad not to find a piece in the royal collections. A few months after our visits a visitor to the musem questioned me about the pattern and told me that he had a lot of it. I half-jokingly said, 'You're lucky, the Queen hasn't got any!' He thought about this and said, 'Do you think she'd like some of mine?' He explained that he had no one to leave it to and, rather sweetly, said that he would be pleased to know that it was going to go to a good home! So I put it to the Lord Chamberlain and the Queen accepted the kind offer. My wife and I went to the owner's Oxfordshire farmhouse and there were pieces of the 'Royal Lily' everywhere – the dog was drinking from one of the bowls. Barbara and I made up two complete services: a dinner service for twenty-four people and a tea service for twenty-four, all the pieces of a date about the time of King George's Worcester visit. The dinner service went to Buckingham Palace and the tea service to Kew Palace where it is used for special occasions and remains on public display when not in use. In return for the gift, the kind donor had an invitation to one of the royal garden parties, which greatly delighted him. Barbara and I were invited to the same party and we saw the Oxfordshire farmer across the crowded lines of people waiting to see the royals as they slowly progressed. It was a lovely day and we had a great time, a lovely tea, a stroll around the grounds and a chance to see the superb Chelsea Mecklenburg Strelitz service in the corner cabinets in the octagon room, which leads out to the gardens. Whether the visitors to the Palace during the summer months dare to stand and stare at the service as I did I know not, but they ought to.

One exciting evening in 1981 we were invited to an evening reception at No. 10 Downing Street, hosted by Mrs Margaret Thatcher. We were invited through friendship with her personal secretary, who was a Worcester resident. We mounted the staircase, past the great row of our Prime Ministers, with my aunt Vivienne's photographs at the top, and were met by Dennis Thatcher, as his wife had been detained in Parliament. There were nibbles and drinks for the large number of guests but the whole evening was very informal, everyone mingling and chatting. When Mrs Thatcher arrived, she and Dennis did a great job of circulating and meeting as many people as possible. The guests ranged from politicians (including Peter Walker, MP for Worcester); sportsmen (Peter West, Dickie Bird the umpire, who was rather nervous and asked us if we would introduce him to Joe Gormley the Yorkshire trades unionist, which we did when we managed to winkle him away from chatting to Margaret Thatcher), entertainers (Terry Wogan, Eric Morecambe and Ernie Wise, Ronnie Barker, Tim Rice, Derek Fowlds of the BBC comedy programme *Yes, Minister*, plus the producers and writers of that programme, which apparently Mrs Thatcher loved), Dame Ninette de Valois the ballerina and lots of ordinary people who had done special things, such as Harry Hirons, the postal worker who had spotted a letter-bomb addressed to MP Mrs Gill Knight. Most of these had their wives or husbands with them and it was especially nice to see the great actress Valerie Hobson with her husband John Profumo.

The evening was a great joy, with everyone mingling; Barbara never forgets being allowed to pull Ernie Wise's hair to see if it was real and not a wig! The high spot for me was having Eric Morecambe slap my chops, just like he did to his partner Ernie Wise on TV. We were introduced to Mrs Thatcher (I had taken her round the factory some years before) and shown the Cabinet Room in which the great decisions of the country are made, and I sat in the Prime Minister's chair for a moment.

In this period son John met, courted and married a wonderful American girl named Kristin. They were introduced to each other at a party in London by her one-time history professor, Angus Johnston of Chicago, who was also a friend of ours and a keen collector of porcelain. The wedding was in Kalamazoo (where they say, 'Yes, there really is a Kalamazoo'). John's brothers, David and Peter, and I sang the music for the wedding service (no, it was not *I've got a girl in Kalamazoo*!) and gave them some real English wedding music: Purcell, Elgar and Wesley. After their honeymoon, spent in America, they returned to live in Kent, producing two lovely children, Elizabeth and Robert.

There were some sad times for us in this period. Both our parents died, after long and happy lives. Barbara came from a large family, with loving brothers and sisters, but I was an only child, so missed my parents very much. They lived long enough to see some of my successes but it made me feel that I must make a few changes in my life, now that the children had left home. The cathedral organist, Christopher Robinson, moved to St George's Chapel, Windsor, and later to St John's College, Cambridge. He was succeeded by Donald Hunt, who came from Leeds Parish Church, and after I had completed twenty-five years in the cathedral choir and sung at the same number of Three Choirs Festivals, I thought it time to finish and devote myself to the Museum, lecturing and broadcasting. Several agents were providing me with lectures that were getting more and more interesting and I continued my lecture tours of the United States.

The Bristol studios of the BBC tried out an idea of taking antiques to the public, inviting people to bring their antiques into a large hall where they would be seen by a group of experts, chosen from auction houses, antique shops and museums. The programme, called *The Antiques Roadshow*, was tried out in Hereford in 1977 and the public were so fascinated with the programme that it is still going strong. In its twentieth season the viewing figures on a Sunday late afternoon were so high that churches were losing their evening service attendances. I will say more about *The Antiques Roadshow* in the next chapter and let you into some of the fascinating behind-the-scenes stories.

The presenter was Arthur Negus and he was so popular with the viewers that the BBC gave him his

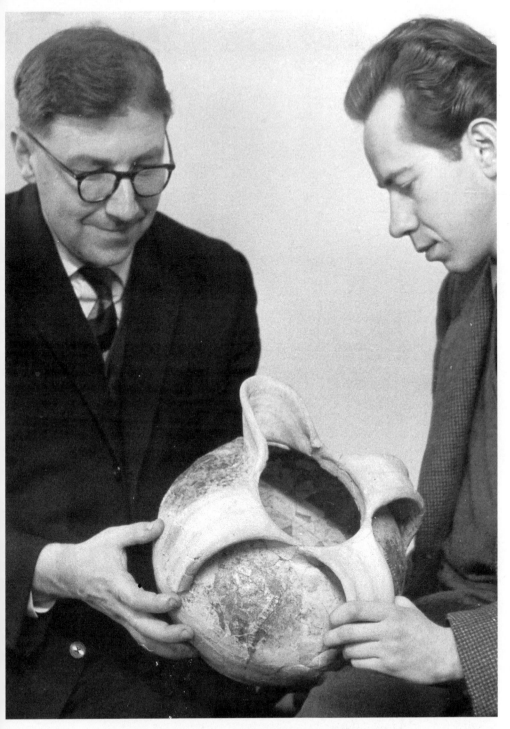

An extremely rare twelfth-century water or wine pot, made in Santoinge-les-Pots and found by me at the bottom of a medieval well in the Lich Street area of Worcester. The huge pot was in 150 fragments, was put together by the British Museum and is now in Worcester City Museum. With me is Maurice Fendall who was on the staff of the Worcester City Museum, 1957.

Our family outside the north door of Worcester Cathedral before attending the wedding of Celia and Roger Humphries, 1968. Our children are, from left to right: Peter, David and John. Celia is the daughter of Hugh Watson, a supernumery lay clerk in the Cathedral Choir, and is also Godmother to John.

Showing the Royal Worcester Doughty Birds to Prime Minister Edward Heath and Worcester MP Peter Walker (later Lord Walker) in the Dyson Perrins Museum, 1972.

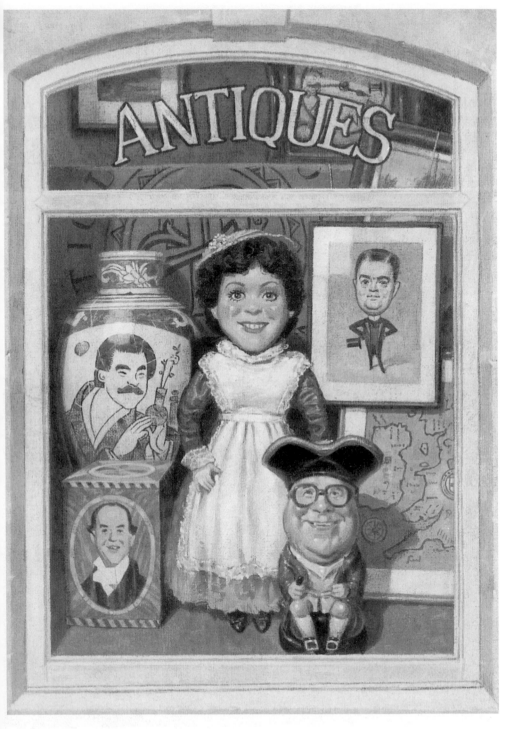

A *Radio Times* cartoon depicting five of us from the BBC *Antiques Roadshow* as objects in an antiques shop-window. Clockwise from bottom left: John Bly as a Georgian tea caddy, David Battie as a Japanese man on a blue and white vase, Hillary Kay as a doll, Hugh Scully as a print and me as a Toby jug. This led Peggy Davies Ceramics of Stoke-on-Trent to make a Toby jug of me.

My great find at the Northampton BBC Antiques Roadshow – Ozzie
the slipware owl who was bought at auction for almost £22,000 by Stoke-on-Trent
Museum. Note my 'Bobby Charlton' hairstyle, which Barbara
insisted was changed in 1994. Photograph © BBC

Caught by Noel Edmunds and presented with a 'Gotcha Oscar', 1992. In the first picture I am inspecting the Minton vase brought in by the 'crooked' actor. In the second I am swearing as I realise I have been stitched up. Photographs © BBC

One of two performances by some of us from the *Antiques Roadshow* team in the live TV charity programme 'Children in Need'. The first year we sang cockney music-hall songs. Here, the following year, we are performing an extract from *My Fair Lady* with me as Dolittle the Dustman. Photograph © BBC

A group from the *Antiques Roadshow* team with Hugh Scully holding the BAFTA award presented to the programme in 1996 for consistent quality over nineteen seasons. Photograph © BBC

My son John and me at the *Antiques Roadshow* outside Waddesdon Manor, 1996.
The public loves to see us together and usually says that he looks and sounds like
me – I tell them that he is a 'chip off the old pot'! Photograph © BBC

The four directors, including myself, of the new ceramic factory Bronté Porcelain
Company of Malvern together with some of the talented craftsmen who are
producing some of the finest ceramics of any time, 1996.

Our family, Christmas 1994. From left to right: (back row) David, Kristin (John's wife), me and John; (front row) Elizabeth, Barbara with Snowie, Robert and Peter.

own programmes. He did a journey up the Great North Road, stopping to talk about some of the interesting places en route. I don't think Arthur was at his best in this – there was not enough of his beloved furniture to enthuse over – but the next series was just up his street. *Arthur Negus Enjoys* was a lovely series and regarded by many as some of the finest television arts programmes ever made. The idea was that Arthur and a guest would look at a couple of rooms in a great house, chatting about a piece of furniture, porcelain or silver that took their fancy. It was a friendly discussion about the qualities and merits of the piece, more time being spent over an item than was possible on *The Antiques Roadshow*. Meanwhile the camera would follow every thought, lingering lovingly on the point being discussed. The programmes, which lasted half an hour, were filmed over two days by a small team. The first one I did was at Littlecote House in Wiltshire and dear Arthur always told people afterwards that it was his favourite programme. As he said in the next one we did, 'People used to stop me in the street and say, "Didn't you and Henry hit it off!"' He really was a wonderful person and as lovable off the screen as he was on it.

The Littlecote programme was made while the Wills family still owned it and we decided to deal with just two of the rooms in this great Tudor manor house. First was the great hall. As Arthur pointed out, it was heavy, dark and strong. We talked about the owner of the house in the time of Oliver Cromwell – Alexander Popham, who had his own private army whose buff-coloured coats, helmets and weapons proudly hung on the walls. Arthur wasn't very good at remembering people's names and facts – after all, he was getting ancient – so I had to pop in bits of information. I explained that Popham had fought against the king in the civil war but helped in the restoration of Charles II and entertained the king with a feast in the very hall in which we stood. We talked about a huge pewter charger bearing the date 1661 and the Latin text 'Vivat Re Secundus', and I mentioned a device of a sun rising in splendour as if the king, like the sun, had returned, and an engraved tulip, which was to be found on delft ware of the time. Of course, the camera showed this in full detail. Arthur talked about the huge table that almost filled this vast hall, which was in fact a games table, a bit like a giant shove-ha'penny board. You had to whack metal discs down the table and score if they stopped between lines, the scoring helped by the discs having letters AA or PP on them (for Alexander Popham).

I said to Arthur, 'I suppose you would have played this game way back in 1660.'

'Hey, I'm not as old as that!' said Arthur. It was that sort of happy camaraderie.

We went on to talk about a pair of huge German salt glaze stoneware Bellarmine jugs, dated 1594, with the coat of arms of Elizabeth I, and therefore contemporary with the hall. I described the method of making salt glazed stoneware and pointed out that in a few years' time the jugs would be four hundred years old. We decided that the jugs looked a bit like us – round and jolly – and it led to Arthur talking about a huge leather bombard which would have held about four gallons of ale. Then Arthur gave a potted history of a group of early English chairs. One chair could have been bought for the great hall when it was built by Sir John Popham and I brought in the fact that Sir John was Lord Chief Justice of England and presided over the trials of Sir Walter Raleigh and Guy Fawkes. The chair was an uncomfortable-looking thing with lots of round knobs and turned bits, and Arthur said, 'These are known as thrown chairs.'

I thought he meant 'throne', so I said, 'Throne – like a queen's throne?'

'No,' said Arthur, 'you should know – thrown, like thrown on a wheel – the wood turned on a lathe,' and he went into a wonderful description of how the wood was turned on a primitive pole-lathe. This was all unscripted and his words came out like honey and his eyes sparkled as he talked about his beloved woods. He was as much in love with wood as I was with pots, and he caressed a veneer as I would a glaze. We finished the first half of the programme under the painting depicting the exterior of Littlecote in 1660.

We recorded the second half of the programme in the drawing room. Arthur explained that we had gone from the heaviness and darkness of the great hall's seventeenth century into the light and colour of the eighteenth century. The room really was dazzling, like a peacock proudly displaying. At first Arthur enthused about the Chinese wallpaper, hand painted with birds in branches. He remembered that when he was young he could never understand how rooms of Chinese wallpaper were sold, thinking at first they had to be scraped off the walls. Then he found out that they were mounted on linen so that they could easily be taken off the walls and transported elsewhere. He pressed the wallpaper, showing how it moved. I drew his attention to a superb pair of Worcester porcelain vases, with pink scale ground, fine gilding and painting of pseudo-Chinese figures in a style called *chinoiserie*, a kind of comic-opera Chinese. On a table was a garniture of three of the most magnificent Worcester vases I had ever seen – pot-pourris for sweet-smelling flowers, encrusted all over with handmade porcelain flowers and ribbons, made and put on by a craftsman called a 'repairer', and I explained that the most famous of them was a man we know to be John Toulouse, who would often put his mark 'IT' or 'To' in the piece – and there were the marks, which the camera picked up. I said they were 'scrumptious', a term which amused Arthur.

'I would call them "snorters", he said, and he started talking about the table they were on, a fine Pembroke, cross-banded in satinwood; and there was a pair of them.

On the other table sat two plates; one was Worcester from a service made for the Duke of Gloucester in about 1770, painted by someone whose name we did not know but who was called the 'sliced fruit painter' after his habit of painting fruit with slices cut from them. I explained that Worcester of that period showed a green translucence – the camera and lighting men were able to show this. The other plate was Chelsea, from a service made for the Duke of Cambridge (when I started to say this, I couldn't remember his name, so I quickly said 'another nobleman'). This had a thicker translucence with white patches, or 'moons', and this was shown. I think this was the first time such a thing had been shown on TV. Arthur moved to a splendid George I walnut card table, with guinea wells for the money. On the top were some of the greatest ceramic treasures of Littlecote – a large group of Worcester plates painted with fable subjects after Aesop or Gay. One depicted Aesop's fable 'The Ass and the Lap Dog', and they were absolutely beautiful. Arthur finished the programme by saying goodbye to the viewers and thanked me for coming. Thank me? Heavens, it was pure joy!

I have described this programme at some length in the hope of showing how wonderful it was to work with Arthur, how generous he was in praising others and also because a lot of the wonderful contents are no longer at Littlecote, so if you want to see them you will have to watch the occasional repeats of the

Arthur Negus Enjoys programmes. The next one we did together was at Corsham Court, the home of Lord Methuen. Barbara came with me on this programme and got on equally well with Arthur. When he found her holding back, he went out of his way to take her into a room, saying that his wife always felt left out and he knew how she felt. A couple of weeks before the recording, we did a recce of the Court on a Sunday morning with the production team, to decide what items we would talk about. Arthur decided to bring his wife Queenie, although she seldom used to go on the visits. He told her she would have a lovely Sunday lunch in the Methuen Arms pub, which the BBC were told would not need booking. When we got to the pub it was jammed full and we had to have bar snacks. Queenie was cross, and I never saw Arthur terrified except on that occasion. They were a happy couple, however, though Queenie's heart was not in antiques. People imagined that they lived in a Georgian house surrounded by Chippendale furniture, but it was actually in a flat, and the only old piece of furniture was something made by Arthur's father. When Queenie died I gave a funeral oration before her ashes were buried with Arthur's and I told the congregation the story of the Methuen Arms lunch and said that I thought I had been asked to say a few words as I was so often mistaken for Arthur that I felt that I had been married to Queenie. It was a cheerful and not a tearful service.

The hardest thing we had to face in this period was

that Barbara developed a breast cancer. In those days such a fact was still terrible and unmentionable, but Barbara is a very strong person and she had the operation. The time after such a thing can be very difficult but we got through it with love and a certain amount of humour.

Shortly after this, in 1982, I was headhunted for the position of director of a new museum of ceramics which was to be opened in Toronto, Canada. I had an interview in London, and Barbara and I were invited to Toronto to meet George Gardiner, who had built up a fine collection of pottery and porcelain in a short space of time and wanted a new museum to house it. The collection covered most of my favourite things – Pre-Columbian Mexican and Peruvian, English delft ware and slipware, German and English porcelain, especially rare yellow ground wares and figures based on the Italian Comedy. A site had been found, opposite the Royal Ontario Museum in a choice part of town, and the position certainly appealed. We would have to move to Canada (the new director had been guaranteed a work permit), and as the financial arrangement seemd in order I said I was interested.

We waited for a week back in Worcester, having already advised the Trustees of the Perrins Museum of the situation, when I had the call to say that I was offered the post, to start on February 1st 1983. Barbara was not overly in favour of us going, but we have always been ready to let fate take us in the direction it wanted, so we agreed. I was to go over and get settled in and Barbara would come later.

Before I left Worcester I recorded a *Down Your Way* programme with Brian Johnston. He did six interviews in Worcester: as well as me, there were recordings in the cathedral, the cricket ground and Elgar's birthplace, and a couple of recordings of local characters, one of whom was 'Honky' Fletcher, a local fish-and-chip shop proprietor who received his name by shouting 'Honk, Honk!' when riding his bike without a warning bell. We all had to choose a piece of music; I wanted the Elgar anthem with my family singing on it, but Elgar had already been taken by the birthplace museum so I picked John McCormack singing 'Il mio tessaro' from Mozart's *Don Giovanni*, explaining that I had admired his voice and the incredible breath control that he displayed in the recording.

The factory and museum put on a lovely farewell. The company directors presented me with some porcelain figures, modelled by James Alder. All my friends in the decorating departments did a painting in a presentation book in the way it was done in pre-war days. The museum staff had a loving-cup painted by James Skerrett with a portrait of Barbara's poodle Snowie. The museum Trustees said I could take a piece from the Museum reserve collection – it was easy to choose the first factory production of Harry Davis – a vase he painted at the age of fourteen, showing a scene of a frozen river Avon below Bredon Hill, which now lives with the same painter's apprentice plate, which was left to me when he died. I am looking at both of these as I write this.

So, Canada, here I come.

6

Television

I arrived in Toronto in the middle of winter, quite unprepared for the cold, with English clothing that really was not suitable. Toronto is a fine modern city with incredibly clean streets and good transport. I soon found a small apartment, a short walk from the site of the museum, and was fixed up with an office in the university. My first task was to meet all the people involved with the planning and building of the museum and to make suggestions for the layout, which was to be on two floors. We worked out that the best arrangement was to put the heavier earthen-wares on the ground floor, lit by strong lighting, with the more delicate porcelain upstairs where daylight or gentle lighting would show the pieces to their best advantage. I was allowed to make lots of suggestions, most of which were happily accepted by the Trustees, such as a glass pyramidal case for the Mexican pieces, a tavern setting to show the delft ware drinking vessels and a theatrical setting to show off the Italian Comedy figures.

I had to sit on various committees, attend lots of meetings, catalogue the collections and decide where each piece would fit into the cases. I founded a

Friends group of keen residents who wanted to play a part in the running of the museum and gave them weekly lectures about the collections. Building works started and we were looking forward to opening towards the end of the year. After a couple of months Barbara came over to stay for a fortnight and help me settle into another apartment, the lease of which I took over from a lecturer at the university. Barbara arrived after the winter had passed and the short period of spring had arrived, so it was quite pleasant and she missed the searing heat of summer, when the temperature often got into the 100s. She would have died to experience that. But she liked Niagara Falls.

The first Sunday I was in Toronto I walked down Yonge Street, which I was told was the longest street in the world, running from downtown Toronto up to the Arctic circle, but I never tried to prove it. I went into the Cathedral of St James, just in time for the end of mattins – a civic service with the national anthem at the end. I was so impressed that I wrote to the organist and offered my services. He jumped at my offer and I sang most Sundays and a few weekday services in a very spirited choir who enjoyed singing; I had a great time, being paid as a deputy, although I was offered a full-time lay clerkship. I also contacted the organist of the large United Methodist church, Melville Cook, whom I had known when he was organist of Hereford Cathedral. It was a great coincidence meeting up again and he asked me to deputise at his church, at first in concerts, then for a

month in the Sunday service choir when the regular
bass wanted to be away. It was great to get back to
some singing, especially in the cathedral, which still
did the full psalms for the day, whereas in many
English cathedrals the wonderful psalms for the day
had been dropped in favour of a short eight or sixteen
verses, which I thought was awful, not to mention
the bringing in of new services with trite words and
even 'clappy-happy' music. I had to go to the colonies
to find real Anglican traditions continuing.

After seven months in Toronto things began to get
rather difficult. Barbara thought it was through my
overworking and the pressures, and I lost a lot of
weight – about four stone, having to have my suits
taken in twice. I blamed it on the great heat of the
summer, a lot of walking and cooking sensibly for
myself. We were about to move the ceramics from
the house to the museum and I had appointed a
couple of assistant curators when there was a parting
of the ways and I resigned. I was sad not to see the
museum open, though the next director lasted a
shorter time than I had and now the museum is
under the auspices of the Royal Ontario Museum. It
was not a happy ending but it had been an interesting
experience and I returned to Worcester rather
deflated and not in the best of health.

For a few weeks I moped about at home. Barbara
looked after me and a loving family helped. This was
the first really rough passage I had experienced, and
I think I came though it a stronger person. I told the

BBC that I was back and offers began to stream in and I got lots of lectures through my agents. Looking back on it I think it did good in the long run, as it certainly got me out of the rut that I had dug myself into and I learned to stand on my own feet, now being self-employed.

The BBC *Antiques Roadshow* had started to take off in a big way. I had appeared in some of the early ones, before I left for Canada, at such towns as Blackburn, Bolton, Derby, Exeter, Folkestone, Gloucester, Leamington Spa, Malvern, Norwich, Oldham and Stoke-on-Trent. As the popularity of the programme grew, the BBC asked Bristol to make more each year. By the time I returned from Canada there were eight different programmes each season. It later rose to twelve; now in 1997 it is twenty-six. The strain was telling on Arthur Negus in his eighties, and he just did a half-day at the show. The growing crowds who came to the programmes loved to see and chat to Arthur and his recordings were wonderful. I remember him talking to a young carpenter, who had a chest full of tools, about the use that his father had put them to.

One calamity was when Arthur dropped a clock which smashed to bits. The owner took it very calmly, saying that it would give him something to do over the winter months in putting it together and Arthur had given him such pleasure over the years that it was an honour to have it broken by him.

An assistant presenter was brought in to help

Arthur. For one year it was Angela Rippon, the BBC newsreader. She was replaced by Hugh Scully and he took over the full presenting when Arthur Negus died. Arthur's death hit us all very hard and there was a proposal to set up a public appeal to raise money for a scholarship, perhaps to help train a craftsman furniture-maker or some such thing, but the producer, Robin Drake, regrettably died as well, so the plan did not go ahead. The new producer, Christopher Lewis, has seen the programme go from strength to strength.

It is hard to say what is the secret of the *Antiques Roadshow*. Basically, it is a simple idea. The public are invited to bring their treasured antiques along to a hall where they are seen by experts who tell them the facts, whether the objects are of little or huge value, whether good or ordinary. Every piece is seen, every person greeted. The most interesting pieces, or something with local interest or which has a fascinating story behind it, are chosen to be specially recorded at a table by three rostrum cameras and the expert tells the unsuspecting but hopeful owner what it is. At the climax, when the value of the object is being built up to, the camera switches to the owner's face to catch the full effect of the valuation – will the owner be shocked, delighted, die? Hugh Scully has rightly described it as a conversation between two people, with fourteen million eavesdroppers.

The programme has not changed a great deal since the early days. What changes there have been have tidied up the programme, making it more helpful to the public by explaining more, so that the viewer is educated. They are recorded a long way in advance of showing, of course, so that the enormous amount shot can be edited down into three quarters of an hour and the close-ups of the particular points that the expert makes can be shown by superb camera work in incredible detail. There are always some people who think that the programme is live. At one time, Hugh Scully would end by saying 'Goodbye from . . . and see you next Sunday in Watford'. Sure enough one irate letter came in from a viewer who said, 'Last week Hugh Scully said "See you next week in Watford," so I went along to Watford and you weren't there.'

Virtually all the recording is done in one day, but a lot goes on before and after the great day. Some days before, the 'furniture round' is done; an expert visits all the people who have written in following adverts in the local media, saying that if they have something too large to bring in, someone will visit them if they send details and photographs. The expert decides if the piece is worth collecting by van and taking to the hall on the day before the recording. I say this to comfort those who worry about the little old lady standing by the huge long-case clock, thinking that she had to wheel it in on a cart. By the day before the recording the hall has been fitted up with the lighting – a massive operation. The screens with photographs of the experts are put in position, and the production staff meet to discuss arrangements for the next day, the two stage managers do some tests with the camera and sound recordists, the recording team make sure that everything is in order, Alec Yirrell gives the local volunteer team details of how they should control the crowds both outside and inside the hall and the police and St John Ambulance set up their stands. There is always a large police presence, not just to look out for any crooks or stolen pieces but also to assist the public, as the *Roadshow* is a great opportunity for them to chat to people about security and protection of their property.

By late afternoon the vans have brought in the big pieces of furniture, which are arranged nicely on a central plinth; the reception desk has been set up at the entrance and the shop is ready with all the goodies for the public – books, mugs, boxed vehicles, T-shirts. When all is in readiness for the morrow, the staff go off to their hotels. The eighteen or so experts arrive at the hotel by the evening and join the production staff and any guests for a drink in the bar at about 7.30; then they go in to dinner. This gives the experts a chance to meet and chat to the special guests, who might be, say, the mayor of the town or the tourist officer who may have helped by organising the hall and advertising the programme. It is a lovely, convivial evening and it must be a comfort to the director that everyone has arrived. The evening ends when he gives a little chat, introducing the guests and giving details of the next day: when the experts should arrive at the hall, whether there is a photocall for some or all of us – a sort of headmaster's lecture. A longer one is given on the first recording date of the season, as there have usually been some changes in the production team since the end of the last season. He will also read out some of the letters that have been received, many addressed to Hugh Scully. They have us in fits:

> Dear Hugh, thank you so much for letting my sister have her photograph taken with you. She said you were busy, yet you offered to go outside with her. Not many would offer to do that. . . .
> P.S. You remind me of Jack Hawkins.

One newspaper said that the *Roadshow* was the only popular programme on TV with no sex or violence in it – one of my colleagues said that the reporter should have been at the hotel after the programme was recorded! (But I always drive home to Barbara.)

The experts' team are a wonderful lot and we have become great friends over the years. At any particular programme there will usually be three specialists in ceramics, two on paintings, two on silver and jewellery, two on toys and clothing, one on clocks and watches, one on books, one on arms and armour, one furniture and four covering all the oddities on two tables known as Miscellaneous, or, as Eric Knowles calls it, 'the owt else table'. If one expert does not know what a piece is, there will almost certainly be another who does, and there is a great camaraderie among us. Many have become household names; when you come into millions of people's living rooms almost every Sunday, they feel they know you, and it is lovely to see the joy in their eyes when they recognise you, even if they usually say to me, 'It's wonderful to see you in the flesh.' There's no answer to that, except to tell them that I'm on a diet.

Among the most recognisable of the *Roadshow* team are John Bly, who is a great furniture expert and the third generation of an antique dealers' firm (and his son has now joined the team); David Battie of Sotheby's, a specialist in ceramics, especially Japanese; Hugo Morley Fletcher, European ceramics; Gordon Lang, Chinese ceramics; Hilary Kay, full of knowledge about teddy bears and pop memorabilia; Bunny Campione, dolls and toys; Paul Atterbury, Victorian and twentieth-century design; Simon Bull, clocks and watches (he turns up either riding a motorbike or driving a huge ancient car); and Eric Knowles, who has become even better known since appearing on the new version of *Going for a Song* and a new antiques programme, *Going, Going, Gone.* Even my son John is getting recognised in the street because of the programme, and the public especially like to see us together on the same *Roadshow* table as they say we look and sound alike – I suppose he is a chip off the old pot!

On the morning of the recording I try to get to the hall by nine o'clock to have a chance to chat to the people in the queue, some of whom have been waiting since dawn. Some bring folding chairs to sit on – the clever ones will have brought a chair to show to the furniture expert and they use it to sit on while they are waiting. All are so delighted to see a face they know, many want an autograph and they really make you feel that you are a famous film star or something. You can usually get some idea of how busy the day is going to be by how long the queue is at that time, though the doors are not due to be opened until almost ten o'clock. When the public are let in they go first to the reception desk where they are given tickets according to the type of antique they have; then they join the queue for the appropriate table, directed by the stewards, headed by John Curry who particularly looks after the ceramic queue, usually the longest. Our tables are especially difficult, not only because so many people bring lots of pottery and porcelain but also because such things are very fragile and have to be handled carefully when being unwrapped and rewrapped. Thankfully there are very few accidents – the experts know how to handle things, but sometimes an old repair will come apart under the hot lights, or the owner knocks a handle or spout off when getting it out of their bag in their excitement. I have found ways of comforting them by saying something like, 'Don't worry, dear – remember that you came in with six pieces and you're going home with seven.' This seems to cheer them up.

The programme allows the public to see and chat to personalities they see on their screens, to see how a complicated programme is put together and to appreciate the amount of work that goes into making what will eventually appear as a thing of seamless beauty. Although many people have to queue for quite a long time there is always something to see – the fine display of brought-in furniture, arranged under the direction of the scenic designer John Bone; the stage managers Dave Brazier and Cliff White directing the customer and expert at the recording table in turn, gathering round behind the table to learn the price that the expert is going to put on the item; seeing how the small roving camera team will pick up a sudden discovery at one of the tables or Hugh Scully chatting to a visitor.

Most of the things that are brought in are just ordinary and are not seen on the finished programme – after all, we can see a thousand pieces each on the ceramic table. But we give all the owners equal respect and time and try to see and value every piece. Though most items have little financial value I always keep in mind that the owner loves it, or it came from Mother or Auntie and so is something special. It is always possible to say something interesting or helpful and send them away happily. I will perhaps say, 'It's not valuable yet, dear, but put it away for a hundred years and I'm sure it will be,' or, 'The contents of the bag aren't very good, but I do like the bag; look after it and don't get it creased and it will be collectable one day.' Off they go, clutching their Tesco bag with joy in their hearts.

Many do not want to know the value. They just want to share the pleasure of the item with you or have some information about it. Sometimes when you tell them that it is of little value they are quite delighted – 'Good, I can go on using it,' or, 'Now I won't have to insure it,' they will say. You get those who won't believe what you say – they may think it is more valuable or older than you say it is, and you have to have the patience of a saint to talk them round. They will say, 'It must be three hundred years old because it belonged to Grandma,' and it has the word 'England' or 'Germany' on it which means that it won't be earlier than 1891 to conform with the McKinley Tariff Act. The most difficult task is persuading them that their swan is a goose – a gold anchor-marked piece is not early Chelsea as Grandad said, but a French or German fake.

The funniest fake I had was a modern 'Roman' lamp, made in the last few years from clear, mass-produced clay. The owner was convinced it must be genuine early Roman: 'I bought it in Italy,' he said. 'They were digging a hole in the ground and as I looked down they found it in the mud, so it must be genuine.' I think I managed to persuade him that the workmen would have had a pocket full of them. If there had been time I would have told him about Billy and Charley who did such things in the Thames mud while digging out Shadwell Dock in Victorian days; their fakes, known as Billys and Charleys, are now worth more than the originals they were faking. Masses of fakes are brought in – modern copies carrying faked reign marks, fakes of antiquities bought in Egypt or Peru. We try to make them understand why we believe they are not old, and comfort them by explaining that they are holding useful learning tools.

I seem to have built up a reputation among the public of being kind to everyone and always having a smile on my face. I always seem to come up with a happy remark to cheer the owner and make the crowds of onlookers laugh. A reporter put in a paper that I said to someone who brought in a rather battered piece, 'This has had a hard life, like me!' I always seem to get the funny fellow who asks, 'How much is my missus worth, then?' I usually say, 'Oh, she's priceless,' which goes down well, but when you get the same question for the umpteenth time you get a bit uptight and once I said, 'It depends where you sell her – if it's in the Middle East she'd be worth seven camels.' The husband took it as the joke it was meant to be, luckily. The *Daily Express* wrote about the Blenheim Palace recording:

The doyen of the experts is former Museum curator Henry Sandon, a twinkly Pooh Bear figure in his seventies [*sic*]. While Oxfordshire hopefuls join the queue for his table he takes as much trouble explaining the merits of a piece of

Goss souvenir china as a priceless Meissen
figurine. 'Keep it in the family,' he says tactfully.
'You love it and that's the important thing.'

Every now and then, of course, out of the bag comes
a real knock-out piece. Although your heart is
pounding with excitement you must not let it show
to the customer, as you want the surprise to come on
camera, if it is recorded. You ask a few off-beat questions to get a little of the background, as the story
behind the acquisition can be illuminating and it is
helpful to ascertain if the owner is a dealer or knowledgeable about the piece, as they will generally not
be chosen. The ideal is to have someone who genu-
inely does not know what it is, who will be surprised
at what you are going to say, or thinks it is one thing
and you will be able to tell them that it is something
else. When happy, you ask the owner if he will be
happy to have it recorded and if so the next step is to
ask the director if he is happy to put it on his schedule
of recordings. If late in the day there may be no room,
or he doesn't think it suitable, but if all is agreed, the
owner is taken into a room and fed coffee and sandwiches, the piece is taken into security until such time
as they are ready for the recording. Then they are sat
down with you and the piece, the stage manager
signals you to start and the item is filmed.

It might help to understand all this if I go through
the recording process of an actual piece. At
Northampton in the Derngate Centre, a young lady

brought in a bag of odds and ends and started getting them out. The first pieces were not important but we have learned to have all the pieces out before starting to comment. From the bottom of the bag came a wrapped-up pottery owl with a detached head. Instantly it hooted at me that it was a rare Staffordshire slipware owl drinking-cup made of red clay and decorated with coloured slips (liquid clay) which had been feathered; it had been made in about 1700 and was in pretty good condition, considering the fragile nature of the material. There was one in Rous Lench Court, one in the Fitzwilliam Museum in Cambridge – oh, my heart sang! But I kept myself under control and said, 'Isn't that fun!'

'Oh, that's Ozzie,' said the young lady.

'Hello, Ozzie!' said I. 'What do you do with him?'

'Oh, I take off the head and put flowers in him on the mantelpiece.'

'I bet he looks nice,' said I.

I told her that I would like to record the things she had brought in and was delighted when she agreed, and I hurried off to the director to have it put on the schedule. The young lady went to the waiting room and Ozzie to security, which left me with an hour or so before recording to try and decide on a value, while the queue of people still poured in. By good fortune son John was one of the experts that day – he had already recorded a slipware dish – and being an auctioneer he is accustomed to sticking out his neck and giving a price, which is very difficult to do when a similar piece has not been up for auction for a long time. I had decided to put a value of £20,000 on it and suggest up to £30,000 for insurance, when the time came for the recording.

Both the young lady and I had been made up (a necessary thing, in my case especially, as the lights are very bright and hot). We were sat on chairs, close together, with the pieces on the table on a rostrum, with a sizable crowd of onlookers behind, and fitted with radio mikes; Dave Brazier, the studio manager, in touch with the batteries of recording machines in the recording room through his microphone, gave me the signal to start.

I briefly talked about the odds and ends, said they were German and, though fun, were not valuable, but then I asked her to tell me about *the* piece – 'Oh, the little owl,' she said. 'It comes from Father.' She did not know more about it than that, but she used it as a flower vase. I picked up the little beauty and said that it was a rare piece of Staffordshire and actually a drinking cup. I explained how you would pour booze from the body into the head cup and you couldn't put it back until you had drunk the cup all up, so it was a nice way of getting drunk. I told her it was made almost three hundred years ago in Staffordshire, and I described the process of feathering the different coloured slips with the end of a feather. I told her it was very rare and I had long wanted to hold one, clutching it in my hands. Had she any idea what it was worth? No. Had she got it insured? No. I asked, 'If someone went round knocking on the door and offered you £50 for it, would you take it?'

'Oh no,' she said firmly.

'What about £100?'

'No.'

'What about £200?'

A little hesitation, then: 'I don't think so.'

'I'm glad about that,' I said. 'Do you want me to tell you how much I think it is worth?'

'Yes,' she gulped.

'Are you sitting comfortably?'

'Yes,' she said, giving a little wriggle in her chair.

'Well, I think it is worth £20,000 pounds' – a gasp from the crowd behind and she sat there stunned – 'and you should insure it for £30,000.'

The camera was on a close-up of her face.

'Good gracious,' she said. 'I brought it in on a bus!' I told her she should take it home by taxi, and that was the end of the first part of the recording. Then came the close-ups of the points I had made; the stage manager had to remember how I had held the piece so that the close-ups were able to fit into the main recording; and there were the 'noddies' to do (the camera looking at her while she listened, gave a nod or two and looked down at the owl but must not speak). Then it was over. I had to go back to my lengthening queue, the lady to go back home, in a taxi provided by the BBC, with two policemen as escort. Apparently when she came up to the door of the house her mother opened it and was scared stiff to see daughter accompanied by two policemen.

'What have you done?' she said.

Back at the Centre, when Hugh Scully did his closing item, he talked about the owl, which was the last, climactic item. He said that he had been watching the recording in another room on a TV monitor. He heard several of the rigging crew discussing what they thought the value was going to be. 'Oh, £50,' said one.

'I think a bit more,' said the other. 'A hundred.'

High said, 'Well, we now know that Henry has put £20,000 on it,' and it made a lovely close to a memorable item as he said goodbye from Northampton.

Like many owners of a sudden and surprising pot of gold, the owner must have had sleepless nights wondering what to do. The problems of keeping such a valuable piece – the risk of burglary, accidental damage, cost of insurance and being driven out of a love for the thing by its value – led her to put it up to auction. We must not give them guidance on what to do, and everything is kept strictly confidential, but it came up at Phillips in London and went for over £20,000, bought by Stoke-on-Trent Museum with the aid of a government grant, so it has gone back to the town where it was made 300 years ago. The auction house generously made no charge to vendor or purchaser because of the very particular circumstances of its discovery and now Ozzie is the pride and joy of the Museum, appearing on posters with the statement that everyone leaves a little wiser after a visit. Son John told me that the day after the programme was shown his phone was red hot with people ringing up to say that they had an owl, like the one on the *Roadshow*, and would he sell it for them. Most of them were not real Ozzies, of course, but, incredibly, three more genuine ones did turn up from people who realised they had one and they have been sold for up to £28,000. I saw one of them in a case at the International Ceramic Fair in London and it had a note saying, 'No, I am *not* Ozzie.'

After the programme, I was stopped in the street by a large number of people wanting to tell me that they had seen Ozzie. It was interesting that all the men thought Ozzie was wonderful but many of the women thought he was ugly – how could I enthuse over such a horrible thing? I came to the conclusion that men like the chunky earthiness of pottery, while women prefer the beauty of porcelain. I certainly love Ozzie and often go to visit him. A fine young potter, Wendy Gill of St Asaph in North Wales, also loves him and has made some marvellous copies, by the same complicated processes, perfect in every detail except that she has to use a lead-free glaze (which is more shiny), as lead has long been banned because of its dangers. Wendy made a new Ozzie for Ozzie's original owner, whom I met by chance at an event I did in Church's china shop in Northampton. She told me that the money realised from the sale of Ozzie was used to adopt and look after orphaned children and that brought a lump to my throat.

Some great discoveries have been made on the *Roadshow* and no doubt there will be many more to come. The BBC have brought out videos of some of the Great Moments such as dear old Nora from Liverpool, who was persuaded by her friend to attend the local *Roadshow* and decided to take in a huge teapot that lives on top of her wardrobe in her Liverpool council flat. David Battie identified it as a rare mid-eighteenth-century punchpot by Whielden and it sold for over £14,000, enabling her to buy her council house. So now she lives rent free and attends some of the *Roadshows*, where we all have a loving kiss from our oldest groupie. A long-lost painting, a masterpiece by Richard Dadd entitled *Artist's Halt in the Desert*, turned up at the Barnstaple *Roadshow*. Painted while the artist languished in Bedlam after killing his parents, it had lain unrecognised for years rolled up in a tube in a Barnstaple attic until it was valued at over £100,000 at the *Roadshow*, subsequently being bought by the British Museum. A great collection of silver, bought a piece at a time by a mad-keen collector using the housekeeping money, was brought into the Crawley *Roadshow* by his son after the silver addict died, and was valued at over £100,000.

People often ask me about the dangers that could arise after the programme is seen by millions of people. Surely the owners could get robbed? I explain that no one except the director knows the name and address of the owner, and that nearly always by the time the item is seen on TV the very valuable pieces have been sold or are in the security of an auction house. The public just seem to love the programme: young and old, rich and poor, even those with little interest in antiques, all love to watch. When a *Roadshow* was interrupted to show live pictures of Nelson Mandela walking to freedom, the BBC switchboard was jammed with complaints. One *Roadshow* hit number three in the Megawatt charts, which register the effect on the National Grid of electricity consumption as people rush to put the kettle on after a favourite show. At Cleethorpes, one man started queuing at four in the morning. A cat painting, bought at a car boot sale for fifty pence, was identified at the Inverness *Roadshow* as the work of the Belgian eighteenth-century artist Henrietta Ranner and was later auctioned for £22,000. A 'witches bottle' found under the doorstep of a house in Wymondham still contained the rusty nails put inside to keep the witches from crossing the threshold and was worth £1,000 even without its handle.

During the season hardly a week goes by without a few words appearing in a newspaper or magazine. Here is a typical piece, written by Marcus Berkmann in the *Daily Mail*:

No programme on television is so utterly quintessentially British. When something really valuable does crop up, the expert plays it cool. He points out the various flaws or cracks in the piece and then comes in with his punchline – five grand or more. Can the contestant restrain the smug smile that is itching to break out? Twelve million viewers move closer to the set. Go on, we shout. Finally a small self-satisfied grin emerges and Britain breathes again. And this is the programme's genius.

In no other country would someone's lack of reaction to good news be considered raw material for top-rated TV entertainments.

But for the contestants it's vitally important to remain dignified, restrained and polite – characteristics the world once regarded as essentially British.

Anyone else would whoop and holler and kiss the nearest stranger full on the lips. On *Antiques Roadshow* they say Good Gracious.

Perhaps that explains why the programme is very popular in many parts of the world. It is seen normally in the Netherlands and Belgium and has been bought and shown by the TV authorities in the USA, Canada, Australia and New Zealand. The programme has been recorded very successfully in Holland and Belgium, Gibraltar and Malta, France and Scandinavia. The farthest distance travelled so far was to Jamaica. I was not fortunate enough to go on that one but saw the lucky experts sitting under sunshades, drinking rum punch, while they saw the strangest things ever brought to a *Roadshow*. The programme had not been seen on local TV so the local populace did not really know the idea and thought the experts were there to buy things from them. So there were piles of pots and pans offered up for sale and little else. But the Belgian *Roadshow* produced a collection of twenty-five Philippine watercolours, later sold at auction for £160,000, so more overseas programmes will certainly happen. The local tourist boards help with the finances of setting up the programme, as they regard it as enormously beneficial in publicising a place. In Great Britain, the only problem is finding a suitable hall, of large size and suitable shape with good facilities and car parking, in which to mount the programme. The majestic town halls of Yorkshire and Lancashire make splendid venues, as do university and public school halls and even sports centres – these may not look very pretty but when they are full of people and a fine display of antique furniture you cannot see the wall-bars or badminton lines.

My favourite venues are cathedrals. Some of our most spectacular programmes have come from Lincoln, Salisbury, Ely and Truro and when the happy crowds flood in it makes me think of how the naves of these buildings would have been used for secular purposes in medieval days. If I had to pick my favourite venue I think it would be Ely. The theme music, normally played by thirteen instruments, had been set to words by the cathedral organist, Paul Trepte, and was to be sung by the choir as the closing

scene. I had known Paul when he was assistant at
Worcester and he very kindly allowed me to join the
Ely choir and sing. The whole programme ended
with the camera on me, singing 'ooo' on a bottom G.
We always have a wonderful time in Ireland and
among my favourite venues there have been Belfast
and Enniskillen in Northern Ireland and Dublin and
Cork in Eire. Perhaps my favourite programmes are
the ones specially for children, which are called 'The
Next Generation' and shown just after Christmas.
Youngsters are so wonderful to talk to – so open – so
long as you do not talk down to them or act superior.
We often find that they know more about their particular passion than we do, be it toys, comics or what
have you.

The only upsetting *Roadshow* I did was at Rochdale
in Lancashire in 1991. I was seated at my table, with
son John on my left-hand side. In the early afternoon,
when I was half hoping that I could slip off to lunch,
a man sat down on my customer's chair and opened
a shoe box which contained a super pot. It was a
Minton vase, painted in pâté-sur-pâté (white slip on
a clay body) by Solon and signed. I nudged son John
and whispered that it was signed and looked perfect.
John whispered back that it must be worth six to eight
thousand pounds. I said to the owner, 'I'd like to
record this,' but he obviously didn't like the idea,
saying, 'I only brought it in to get a value, as I want
to buy it for my sister,' he said. I talked to him gently,
explained that I would very much like to record it,

that it would all be anonymous, no one would know who he was and at the end of the chat I'd tell him the value. I must have hit the right spot because, a little grudgingly, he said he would do it. I thanked him and was about to arrange for the recording, when Alex Yirrell asked if I would go and see the director. I excused myself to the man, said I wouldn't be long and he put the lid back on the box as I went off.

Christopher Lewis introduced me to a detective chief inspector who said he was from the Serious Crimes Squad and showed me a warrant card with his photograph on it.

'What's the man been saying?' he asked. I told him of his request to have a price on the pot so that he could buy it for his sister.

'We've been very suspicious of him all morning,' said the policeman. 'We've got some enquiries still to do – will you go back and keep him talking and find out all you can?' Me – I ask you!

I went back, all of a tremble, and found the man still on his seat with the covered box in front of him. I tried to keep calm and chatted about the pot and Rochdale and anything else that wasn't too personal, as he was getting a bit agitated and his hands were shaking – not that mine were much better. A lot of people were gathered around. They seemed to sense that something unusual was going to happen. Then something did.

A uniformed Bobby came and stood to my right – I could just see his uniform out of the corner of my eye as I was keeping my attention on the man. 'I'm arresting you,' said the Bobby, in best P. C. Plod accent. (On reflection, the accent was more West Country than Lancashire.) The man jumped up, knocked the box onto the floor, where it fell with a crash, as my heart sank into my boots. The man ran off towards the main staircase of the Town Hall, scattering people.

The Bobby said, 'Don't worry, sir, we'll pick him up downstairs.'

I could not move but just sat there stunned, thinking of the pot. The Bobby said, 'I think it's broken, sir.' I nodded. He picked up the box and started rattling it, presumably to see if it was smashed. This roused me into action and I said, 'Don't do that, you'll make it worse.' I turned to the Bobby, who was grinning like the dog in the psalms, and saw with horror that it was Noel Edmunds, holding a 'Gotcha Oscar' and realised that I had been stitched up. I swore and tried to strangle him. The swear-word was beeped out of the showing of my stupidity when the *Noel Edmunds House Party* was done, so I don't know what I said but I hope it was really good. They told me that the box had been switched while I was away, and the beautiful Minton vase was undamaged, which mollified me a little but I was in a dreadful state all afternoon. I found out that son John had been in on the act all along. They had asked him if I would not mind getting stitched up.

'Oh, no,' said John. 'He's a jolly good sport.'

'Will he have a heart attack?'

'Oh, no,' said John. 'He's perfectly fit.'

Blasted kids: you bring them up as well as you can and they let you down. But even he had not seen them switch the box, so he thought the Minton vase had been smashed, and was as upset as I was. Serve him right!

I suppose it was a horrible trick to play on a pota-holic and when I got home Barbara said that I looked terrible and she thought I had been in an accident. I suppose I had in a way. A month later I had to go up to Television Centre in London and have the Oscar presented to me, live on TV, in the *Noel Edmunds House Party*. I had to watch the recording of me being a stupid fool and they asked me to look happy while I watched and then I was given the Oscar. In those early days of the *House Party* the BBC called the objects Gotcha Oscars and the shape looked somewhat like the American film Oscar. The Oscar Committee objected and the BBC changed the shape and colour and amended the name to Gotchas.

Being on the *House Party* was great fun, as it was live TV. It is always exciting being involved in live TV, when anything can go wrong, especially on such a complicated programme, and it needs someone like Noel Edmunds to keep things going with apparent smoothness. Sitting there, waiting to go on for my bit, it was nerve-wracking to see the thing threatening to fall apart, to be in danger of running late and then just managing to hang together and finish dead on time in a blaze of glory. There could be sheer panic behind the scenes but the viewer must always feel that everything is under control. As I went home that night, carrying Gotcha Oscar and a bottle of 'gunge' from the gunge tank (I wasn't gunged but I wanted a bottle for my grand-daughter), I felt quite proud of myself. I was certainly a hit when I went to my granddaughter's school and talked about my Gotcha Oscar, and for months we had a procession of youngsters coming up to our house to see it – I had to put it in the window, to avoid too much disturbance.

A number of other live TV programmes came my way. The greatest fun was when six of us from the *Roadshow* team were asked to appear on the annual charity spectacular from the TV Centre in aid of Children In Need, the special BBC charity. With me were Hugh Scully, John Bly, Eric Knowles, Bunny Campione and Marge Cooper. The first year we were asked to sing a group of Cockney music-hall songs, dressed as Cockneys, around a wheelbarrow. We were provided with a tape of the songs and a script, the act lasting about five minutes. We did a couple of rehearsals with the choreographer at the BBC rehearsal studios in North Acton, went to the costumiers to get kitted out and were ready for the performance, with six professional dancers to help us to look reasonable. I was happy with the singing and the Cockney of course, but drew the line at doing the high kicks requested.

'Could I just do a knees-up instead?' I asked. 'Much more authentic!'

'Oh, all right,' they said, and it actually went quite well. Our old-time medley was 'Any old iron?', 'Where did you get that hat?', 'Oh, what a beauty!' (the vegetable marrow song), 'A ruin that Oliver Cromwell knocked abaht a bit' (my big solo), 'Mr grandfather's clock', a spoon break by John Bly, who was a great performer on Georgian silver spoons, 'Don't dilly dally on the way' and, to end with, 'Knees up Mother Brown'.

I was out of breath after the knees-up and was full of admiration for the wonderful professional dancers, who flung themselves about for the eight hours of the whole night's performance plus the morning and afternoon rehearsals. I had watched most of the rehearsals and thought it tremendous, especially when I saw that the contestants in *The Generation Game* were going to have to do the fiendish lambada dance with Bruce Forsyth. The contestants were footballer Bobby Charlton and quizmaster Bob Holness and their daughters. They had no idea what they were going to have to do, as they had not been allowed to watch the rehearsal. In the Green Room, before they went on, Bob asked me if I knew what they had to do and hoped it would not be dancing.

'Oh no,' I assured him, 'it's just the potter's wheel.'

I watched their performance on a TV set and when Bob realised he had to do the lambada, his face was a picture. There were so many famous people, all giving their time and talents for the great charity, and they all mingled happily in the Green Room. Frank Bruno, the boxer, who had been doing *A Question of Sport*, allowed me to punch him in the stomach – my hand hurt for days. As the total money raised headed towards twenty million pounds, I was as proud as a peacock.

The following year we were invited back again, to an abridged version of *My Fair Lady*. John Bly had to drop out because of the death of his father, but the rest tackled a much more difficult job than the previous year. The other four were dressed beautifully for the Ascot scene, while I had the part of Dolittle the dustman and had to emerge from a dustbin – the producer said it was typecasting. It was thrilling singing 'I'm gettin' married in the mornin'' and 'Win a little bit of luck' to the brilliant band conducted by Ronnie Hazlehurst, and I even got my famous knees-up into the act. Afterwards I chatted with John Dankworth and his wife Cleo Laine (there's name-dropping for you!) who thought it had gone well and, as it was one of their favourite shows, that pleased me a lot. Afterwards I waited for offers to do the part of Dolittle on the stage on tour but they haven't come in yet – agents take note. I spent an hour on the charity phone-in lines. This was a bit scary and took enormous concentration, sitting in a great bank of seats with a phone on my head and a pad in front of me. As the light came on, a new person was on the line, from anywhere in the country, and I had to write down on the form the name, the amount of donation and the way it was raised and get the credit card number down correctly. That was the hardest job – I have never had a credit card as Barbara says I would only use it to buy more pots – so the dreadfully long numbers took my by surprise. I hope I got them down correctly, so if anyone got debited with an amount they shouldn't have that night, they can blame it on me.

The phone-in was an eye-opener. There were so many generous people out there and as I filled up the forms and asked them for details many recognised my voice, which was nice. Famous people were taking their places by the phones all the time and it struck home how generous actors and stars are with their time in aid of charity. At one time I had a moment to look around – on my right was Dinsdale Landon and I shyly told him how much I enjoyed his many light comedy appearances in films and on TV. Then – horror – he said how much he admired me on the *Roadshow*. On my left was little Charlie Drake, answering the phone with his famous catch phrase, 'Hello, my darlings!' and I was in my seventh heaven. If there is an eighth heaven then I was in it next, when I looked down in front of me, for there was Barbara Windsor, the great 'Carry On' comic actress (now a stalwart of *EastEnders*), and I promise you it is all her down there, because I was in the right place to be sure. What a night! Our singing came on in the cabaret hour – after one in the morning – and after that we partied in the Green Room, heard the final total and went on to several other parties, where the professional dancers were still dancing. About 4 a.m. I crept away to the bowels of the TV Centre and slept for a couple of hours in Sarah Greene's dressing-room – she wasn't there at the time, of course, as *Blue Peter* was not until the next Monday.

Many other television offers came in. I did a large number of *Heirlooms* for Anglia TV in Norwich with John Bly, who presented them. They were a little like a mixture of the *Roadshow* and *Going for a Song*, with a small studio audience, some of whom brought pieces for discussion, and the guest was encouraged to present some of his own special treasures, talk about them and give reasons why they were good. I presented ideas such as candle extinguishers, how to tell the genuine from the fake and how modern well-made ceramics can be the equal of those made in the past; and the producer, Colin Eldred, liked me to bring a large touch of humour into the programme. So I showed a curious Mexican figurine that was a drinking pot, but you had to drink from a most interesting place, and the Royle self-pouring teapot that doesn't have to be picked up to pour; they even allowed Barbara's poodle Snowie to appear and do a trick that I had taught him – my father would have been proud of me. The programmes were shown on weekday afternoons to sizable audiences, considering the time of day.

I appeared on *Club X* for Channel 4. The BBC

Roadshow PR asked me to do it and said it was an arts programme and I was to go to the studio in a converted warehouse by Lambeth Walk to talk about souvenirs of the Grand Tour. I collected a number of fine examples brought back from Italy and Greece in the nineteenth century by British travellers but when I got there I found that what they really wanted was the cheap seaside souvenirs of the Edwardian age – Goss and German fairings. *Club X* was a very strange programme which ran from 11 p.m. to midnight once a week, with a young and very merry audience who were let in half an hour before the programme started. I was interviewed by a transvestite, at least that's what he or she told me he or she was. They had brought up from Weymouth a noted sand modeller, who had to build his fine sand pictures while naked girls writhed around on the sand. I was very embarrassed and was somewhat ashamed to be on the programme but I don't think my friends saw me, although I went up in the estimation of the *Roadshow* technical people, to whom *Club X* was a cult programme.

Another strange appearance I did was with Zig and Zag on *Big Breakfast*. This was a rather crazy programme but it was fun working with these two puppets and their brilliant Irish manipulators in the tiny bathroom in the lock-keeper's cottage where the programme is filmed. I had to teach Zig and Zag how to be experts on the *Antiques Roadshow*, in a week in which the puppets had to learn to be experts on different TV programmes. It was interesting to see Bob Holness there teaching them to say, 'Can I have a P, Bob?' in his word-game programme, and I reminded him of when he did the lambada at the Children in Need event.

I still went on trips to America to lecture, particularly at the beautiful house and gardens in Nashville, Tennessee, called Cheekwood, the one-time home of the founders of Maxwell House coffee, the Cheeks. They had a fine collection of the Worcester Doughty birds and I lectured about them. We got on very well and they invited me to be curator from a distance, building up the collection with fine early and middle period Worcester porcelain, so that now they have one of the few collections in America that covers the whole history of Worcester. I went there to lecture most years and would fit in a few lectures in the South, staying with the blue-and-white collector Larry Branyan in Natchez, an old and beautiful town on the Mississippi. I paid visits to Milton and Jeanne Zorensky of St Louis, who had built up the most glorious collection of early Worcester porcelain imaginable, many of the pieces having come from the Rous Lench sale (I had taken both of them to meet Tom Burn at Rous Lench Court). Son John joined with the London dealer Simon Spero to publish a fine catalogue of the collection. A happy lecture was in Washington at the major antique fair where I gave the keynote lecture and I picked the subject 'The British influence upon American collections and collectors'. I always like to have a bit of fun with the Americans and I told them that the original title was 'The American influence upon British collections and collectors' but I could not think of anything, except the Cabbage Patch doll.

Other great American collectors that I have known include the late Henry Clay Hofheimer of Norfolk, Virginia, whose collection has gone to his local museum; Joseph Handley, who lived in an incredible house perched on the edge of a rocky promontory overlooking the Pacific at Big Sur, California, with a fine collection of black printed porcelain about which he published a useful book; a dear couple, Priscilla and Kenneth Klepser of Seattle, who were competitors of Dyson Perrins when he was acquiring early pieces of Bristol/Worcester porcelain from the dealer T. Leonard Crow of Tewkesbury in Gloucestershire. I was so impressed with the collection and the wonderful letters from Crow to Klepser from 1948, which not only talked about the porcelain but dealt with all aspects of British life in those difficult days just after the war, that I felt they ought to be published. Simon Spero produced a fine book about the collection and the letters and I wrote a foreword for the book. There was Dean Rockwell who ran the Mid West Ceramic Study Group, to whom I talked on a number of occasions in Detroit. He brought a party over to Britain every other year, which Judy Watts and I would conduct around an area by coach, visiting museum and private collections, gardens and historic sites over a two-week period. These were great fun, although exhausting, and I had to talk on the coach, telling them what we were coming to and also anything of interest, such as the rules of cricket (you try doing that!), persuading them to look out for fast-flying haggis in Scotland, Welsh rabbits in Wales and Cornish piskies. After four tours of Hadrian's Wall, a dash to Stonehenge and on to Lands End for them to look out to America (I think that was all in one day), I decided that someone younger should do it in future and the task fell to Robert Copeland.

I did some exciting lecture tours of Holland for the Netherlands/England Society. Travelling by train in Holland is so easy that it was a great joy to start off with a lecture in Amsterdam and each day go on to a different fascinating city. So many people speak perfect English there – they say that no one can be expected to learn Dutch – and the subject we chose was the Glorious Revolution, dealing with the change that came over English ceramics following the crowning of William of Orange and Mary in 1689. This led to England following Queen Mary's fascination with blue and white, Dutch delft and Chinese porcelain and the desire to make pottery and porcelain in the same style. It certainly was an interesting period and I explained how all the great houses of England aped the China Mania started by Queen Mary. I enjoyed these tours and even managed to find some Worcester blue and white tea wares of 'Fence' pattern from the 1770s in an antique shop that John told me I had to look out for and buy, which I did.

In the 1980s sons John and David collaborated with me on the production of *The Sandon Guide to Royal Worcester Figures*, a book dealing with the simpler figurines that Royal Worcester made between 1900 and 1965. Many illustrations were of pieces in Barbara's own collection, so it was very much a family book, although Barbara later sold her collection at Phillips.

The last decade of the millennium was to come.

7

Songs of Praise

The 1990s produced a growing volume of requests for broadcasts, lectures and charity appearances that threatened to get out of hand. My television appearances brought in their wake such a deluge of requests that we just had to trim them down. We tried to restrict charity talks and appearances to three main fields – children, cancer and arthritis, the first purely out of affection for the little brutes and the knowledge that we had a family to be proud of; the second because of Barbara's cancer, which, thank God, had been completely cured; and the third because Barbara had arthritic knees and I had arthritic hips. To these we added as many others as we could – the hospices when friends and relations had had help and support; charities which looked after the elderly, such as Age Concern; churches that were in desperate need – oh, there were so many needy things that before we knew what was happening we were doing a hundred a year, often fitting one in en route to a paid job or doing two or three in a day. After a couple of years of this we just had to be more cautious about taking things on. I had to tell different branches of the same organisation that they would have to merge and I would do one big event to raise thousands rather than ten raising a hundred pounds each. The spirit was willing but the flesh began to get a bit weak.

As well as continuing to serve on the Choir Benevolent Fund, I am vice chairman of the Commemorative Collectors' Society, president of the Worcester branch of NADFAS and patron of a dozen or so societies and groups, such as the Evacuees Reunion Association. Requests for lectures poured in, especially from a new agent, Brian Durkin, who ran an agency called BDA in Cheshire. He had some great names on his books and I found myself doing one-man shows titled 'An Evening with Henry Sandon' in some great theatres the length and breadth of the country. I often found myself following or preceding such great stars as Ken Dodd and I really thought I had arrived at last. My shows were in two halves. In the first I would show slides covering my life from early London days up to the TV programmes, popping in stories and even singing songs. At the end of the first half I told the audience I had trained Snowie the poodle to do a trick – if they applauded, Snowie would run up onto the stage, jump into my arms and kiss me on the ear. This brought the house down and sent the audience off to their refreshments in a jolly spirit. The second half was a kind of *Roadshow* – I looked at pieces the audience had brought, chatted, told stories and answered questions.

The *Roadshows* and other lectures were getting me

criss-crossing the country. Once, in Colchester, there occurred the greatest surprise of my life. I got to the town in the afternoon of 2nd April 1992 after a very long drive, ready to talk to the local Antiques Collectors' Club in the evening. Barbara always likes me to let her know when I arrive, so I rang her from a public phone box outside the post office and she was in a real state. She said she had had Buckingham Palace on the phone and they wanted to speak to me. As it was the day after April Fool's Day they stressed that it was quite genuine and gave her the number. I told Barbara that I could hardly ring the Palace from a phone box outside Colchester post office with someone knocking on the door wanting to use it. I asked her to ring the Palace and see what they wanted and I would ring Barbara again. When I rang back, Barbara had contacted the Palace again, to be told that the Queen had invited me to lunch and could I telephone and confirm it the next morning. I told the Club members that evening and received a cheer – someone said that they would put a blue plaque on the phone box. When I got back to Worcester in the early hours of the morning I found Barbara still in a state so neither of us slept much.

I rang the Palace and said that I would be delighted and honoured to come to lunch on 13th May 1992. Would the invitation include my wife? No, just me. 'Oh dear,' said Barbara, 'never mind.'

An invitation came in the post next day, which made it clear it was not a leg-pull, as I had been thinking it was going to be another Gotcha Oscar. I had a month to prepare and, not knowing what to expect or how I should behave, I wrote to the Lord Lieutenant of Hereford and Worcester, whom I had got to know well, and enlisted his help – what should I wear? How did I address the Queen and the Duke? Did I take a present of flowers or chocolates or something – even biscuits for the corgis? I had a lovely letter back, answering all my worries and saying that I would have a wonderful time. I kept it rather quiet, of course, but did tell my granddaughter, Elizabeth, who is half American. I said, 'Grandad is going to have lunch with the Queen.'

'Oh, Grandad,' she said, 'will you be going to McDonald's?' I suppose to her that was the greatest place to go.

I set off very early on the morning of the lunch. Having been sent instructions to arrive at 12.50 p.m., with a nice car pass to be put on the windscreen, I was determined not to be late, not to risk the little roads through the Cotswolds but to belt down the M40 motorway and ensure I was there in time. Of course, I got to London hours early. As I drove down Birdcage Walk I could see that there was a changing of the guard going on; there were huge crowds and I did not know what to do. A kindly policeman suggested that I drove round the side of the Palace where the police have a little place and explain my dilemma. They let me leave the car there while I went to Victoria to have a coffee, returning in time to collect the car and drive in through the main gates, receiving a smart salute from the guardsman. I felt very important. I parked in an area by the side of the Palace, where you sometimes see processions of coaches turning up; I went inside and handed in my invitation.

There was a total of ten people invited for lunch. As we waited in the reception room we chatted rather shyly, probing to find out why we had been invited – no one seemed to know. After a few minutes we were collected and led along miles of corridors into a fine drawing room where we were to wait for the Queen and the Duke of Edinburgh, but they were running a little late owing to a presentation. I had plenty to look at – a cabinet of the finest Sèvres porcelain I had ever seen. I was about to work out a value when the doors were opened, four dogs came bounding in and there were the Queen and the Duke. We were arranged in a semicircle and were introduced by the Master of the Household, shaking hands, giving a little bow, saying 'Your Majesty' at first, then 'Ma'am' when she spoke. It was a lovely, friendly start and the two corgis and two dorgies (a cross between the Queen's corgi and Princess Margaret's dachshund) were around everyone's feet. One made a special fuss of me and I think he could smell Snowie, Barbara's poodle. I was just a little concerned, as I know they can be a bit snappy and I wondered what I would do if he bit me. But the Queen beamed and said, 'He likes you,' so all was well.

The Queen and the Duke, preceded by the dogs, led the way into the dining room, which was named the 1844 Room, presumably the date it had been constructed. The table was a long oval and the Queen and the Duke sat in the middle, opposite each other. The ten guests were from different fields, chosen so that the Queen would have the experience of meeting a range of people. A seating plan gave their names and positions: Prof. Lesley Rees, Dean of Bart's Hospital Medical Centre; Mrs Joyce Rose, Chairman of the Council of the Magistrates' Association; Dr Walter Baker, Chief Executive of the South London Business Centre; The Lord Camoys, Deputy Chairman of Barclays de Zoete Wedd; Christopher Gorringe, Chief Executive of the All England Lawn Tennis and Croquet Club; Rev. Dominic Milroy, Headmaster of Ampleforth College; Vice-Admiral Sir James Weatherall, Marshall of the Diplomatic Corps; Robin Kernick, Clerk of the Royal Cellars; and myself, described as a ceramics expert. I sat between Robin Kernick on my right and Mrs Rose on my left and had been told by the Lord Lieutenant that you were expected to talk to the person on one side for one course and to the other for the next course and this seemed to work well.

The menu was set before each of us and was in French:

Croquettes de Fruits de Mer
Sauce Newburg

Selle d'Agneau Duborg
Mange-tout Flamande
Pommes Château
Salade

Sorbet aux Barbadines

Les Vins: Château Rahoul 1987
Château Calon-Ségur 1970
Royal Vintage 1955

The Queen and the Duke were served first and I think we all looked to see how much they put on their plates and tried not to take more. The food was delicious but I think we were all rather cautious of taking too much. I was pleased to see that the china service used was Minton – I didn't even have to turn over a plate to know that. I asked one of the waiters if the old keeper of the china pantry that we had met was still in service, but was told that he had retired. The glass was beautiful English cut glass. I got on very well with the Clerk of the Royal Cellars and we talked about Malvern water, which the Queen drinks, preferring still to sparkling. I said that we got it direct from the wells on the hills; I even offered to bring a few barrels up to the Palace, which made him laugh.

The meal ended with dessert fruit and cheese, and we all moved for coffee into the magnificent room where we had first met the Queen. The Queen and the Duke made a particular point of talking to those who had not sat either side of them and I found her so friendly and relaxed that I was instantly put at ease. I found out that she watched the *Antiques Roadshow* occasionally and enjoyed it, so I invited her to the Kensington *Roadshow* recording, which was in a few months' time – she could bring something along. She said she would try but couldn't promise. I told her what my granddaughter Elizabeth had said about us dining at Macdonald's, and she laughed. We talked about children, dogs and Sèvres porcelain and the time went so quickly that before I knew it the Queen and the Duke were making their farewells. We waited behind for a while, having more coffee. Then we were taken out down the miles of corridors, told how we could write our thank-you letters so that the Queen would see them personally, and then I drove out of the gates, feeling very important when the guard presented arms and some tourists took photographs. I went home with my head ringing with memories of the wonderful day.

The BBC started a new series of antiques programmes, called *The Great Antiques Hunt*, and these have become an off-season alternative to the *Antiques Roadshow*, to keep the addicts happy until the next season of *Roadshows* comes on the air. It begins with the contestants being given some BBC money, set to buy a particular type of antique at a fair or market, and at the end of the programme sell it themselves at auction. If they make a profit this is added to the points they score in the games. They can be asked to do anything – identify, date or value something, decide whether a piece is genuine or fake, pretend to be experts at an antiques roadshow, show someone around a stately home, spot the wrong item in a period room – oh, anything. The winning pair have their choice out of six antique items, five of them worth about £200 each and one, the star prize, being about £1,000, and they are given just thirty seconds to make their choice. The various competitions are adjudicated by an expert, who gives them a bit of guidance, especially on how to handle an auction, which is a real one, with real dealers and collectors buying, so it is quite a frightening thing to do for the first time.

Presenting the programme is Jilly Goolden, the frizzy-haired blonde who is the wine expert on the BBC food and wine programme. She is a wonderfully lively personality, who is there to put the sort of questions to the experts that ordinary people would like to ask. She is accompanied in the opening scenes by a huge bloodhound, the idea being that the blood-hound is there to sniff out the bargains. I have appeared on the programme at such venues as Bath, Newark, Glasgow, Exeter and Belfast. At Worcester the competition was set in the Dyson Perrins Museum (now renamed the Museum of Worcester Porcelain) and involved the contestants telling genuine Worcester from fakes; at Harrogate they had to date and value teapots in the famous Betty's tea-shop; at Cirencester there were two pairs of teenaged contestants, lively as spring lambs, and when I told the contestants that they had chosen the top prize (two wonderful pots made by craftsman potter Alan Caiger-Smith that I coveted myself) they whooped for joy, jumped up in the air and gave each other 'high fives' (I think that is the term). Then they offered to sell me the pots!

Barbara often comes with me on the *Great Antiques Hunt* and brings Snowie, who is always made very welcome. Once in South Wales he deputised for the bloodhound at the old Nantgarw porcelain factory. He was certainly a lightweight when he jumped onto my lap, and he didn't slobber like the bloodhound. It is always nice when Barbara can accompany me, especially when it involves staying away, as she is a great help in so many ways. She helps at general talks when people bring things in for me to see, passes pots and demonstrates the ones I take myself, such as the new Cadogan teapot that has been made with my portrait on the front. As my 'assistant' she is a great sport and it makes the audience laugh when I refer to her as 'The Beautiful Samantha'; she is especially helpful on our annual lecture cruise for P & O. These Antique Theme Cruises are enormous fun. We have an organiser, Arnold Burman, and two experts. Mostly I have been with Eric Knowles and we have a wonderful rapport. Each of us gives slide lectures and antiques teach-ins while the ship is at sea and we are then free to go on shore when the ship is in a port. We have had the chance to see places that we have dreamed about – Florence, Rome, Venice, Monte Carlo – and I have even helped in taking coach parties to these places. You have to count them on and off again so that you don't leave anyone behind, though I did once – left a lady behind at a waterfall way up a mountain in Norway. I hope she has got back by now.

On several of these cruises I had growing problems with an arthritic hip and Barbara with the even worse problem of a badly smashed ankle. The accident happened at a charity talk that we were giving in January 1995. She was on the platform taking pieces from the audience (they were making donations to the charity for me to look at them) when the platform collapsed under her and she ended on the floor with a broken ankle. She was taken by paramedics to Kidderminster General Hospital, where the ankle was operated on and pinned, put in traction and then plaster. She was in hospital for several months and it was a relief when she was allowed home, although she still had a huge plastered leg and was in a lot of pain. I had to make up a bed-settee downstairs (we live in a semi with the bedrooms and bathroom upstairs) and I had to sleep on the floor as help was needed night and day. We got through, though her foot is still a problem and walking is difficult for her.

I managed to carry on with all my obligations thanks to the help of family and friends. Like all things sent to try us, they trail some benefits in their wake. You grow closer together and discover that there are wonderful friends and organisations bending over backwards to help. Good can come out of bad. These thoughts helped me when I was asked to present a number of the long-running BBC series *Songs of Praise*. I remembered singing in one of the programmes in the choir of Worcester Cathedral back in 1967 when the BBC asked me to present my first one and I was able to run down a copy in the archives of the cathedral. The BBC showed an excerpt when I did the first presentation and sons David and Peter were in the choir and Barbara and John in the congregation, all looking much younger.

The first *Songs of Praise* that I presented was in Arundel. The idea was that it should be an antiques *Songs of Praise*. The producer, Diane Reid, who had been an assistant producer on the *Antiques Roadshow*, had lined up an interesting group of people for me to interview. We visited Arundel Castle and I talked to the Duke of Norfolk and his daughter-in-law. This was particularly interesting as I got the chance to handle some incredible things, such as Mary Queen of Scots' rosary, which she took to the scaffold, and we filmed an early Bible in the library. The Duke was descended from a saint and several cardinals and is the senior Roman Catholic layman in the land. We filmed in Arundel Cathedral and I was shown the Treasury, full of wondrous gold and silver vessels. I asked a pointed question: 'Why shouldn't all these be sold and the money given to the poor?' and got a very reasoned reply, that the money raised would not go very far and that the religious love that had gone into the making and buying of them was proof of the need of Christians to keep such beauty. I was shown the leg of the blessed saint from whom the Duke is descended and learned that a piece was sent to a Roman Catholic church consecrating a new altar, into which the piece of bone is cemented. I was asked if I would like to remove a piece, but I made my excuses and left. It was rather strange to me – a very low Church of England person – but I could understand the religious fervour behind it.

We filmed in a church in Goring-by-Sea whose ceiling was painted with a complete copy of the Sistine Chapel ceiling in Rome, a little smaller in size but closer to your eye as you sat in the seats, with acres of naked flesh floating just above you- – rather distracting, I thought. I interviewed a dear lady who had collected a hundred Bibles and was surrounded by them in her little house. Arundel is a great antiques town and I met someone who collected donated things and auctioned them, the money raised being used to buy Bibles for the Third World. These interviews were interspersed with hymns sung by the local congregations in the Great Hall of the castle, where we had earlier recorded an *Antiques Roadshow*.

The whole thing was great fun but I found that presenting a programme was very different from just being an expert cog in an antique wheel. The presenter has to memorise long 'pieces to camera' (or

PTCs as BBC initials call them), speeches written by the producer, full of names, dates and facts, and it is hard to memorise them and present them with feeling, sometimes while having to walk along a path. You get a bit tongue-tied, trip over a word (or the path), get a date wrong, and then of course you have to do it again. Or you can be standing on the bridge over the river Arun, giving the closing words, and a huge lorry goes by or someone recognises you and wants to chat. So that means another take.

I asked Hugh Scully for some tips on how to present – he does it so well. He said that he insists on writing most of the words himself; then it feels so much more natural. I found that the most successful PTC I did was the last one, so I must be improving, but then I wrote the close myself. It was outside the wonderful cathedral in Dornoch, in the north of Scotland. This was the New Year *Songs of Praise* of 1997. I had to say my close after interviewing some fascinating people – a crofter, a reformed alcoholic who became a priest and teaches classes to speak the dying Gaelic language and taught me to say 'A Happy New Year' in Gaelic, phonetically – 'Bleana var oor'. I had to stand outside a floodlit cathedral on a freezing cold night, and it is etched in my mind, as it was all my own words: 'Like the Magi of old, I made a long journey here to find a Christian spirit of hope and help in this sparsely populated yet beautiful land. Surely God's hand is here, and I hope you have been as spiritually uplifted as I have. From

Sutherland, a joyful new year – Bleana var oor.' The right length, as it had to fill a particular times space and in one take – my joy was complete.

I have presented a number of *Songs of Praise* programmes and found them both fascinating and moving. Some of the people you interview have had great problems with health, family break-ups and disasters, and were knocked back on their heels. But with spiritual help they were able to come to terms with all that life had thrown at them. I was amazed at how they would open their hearts to you, let you into their innermost secrets and confide as if to an old friend. I only felt like crying at the many sad stories and laughing at the many funny ones I heard, and I know how the programmes help millions of viewers by sharing this with them and allowing them to join in the hymn singing, as so many people are unable to attend church. Many of the programmes have been sold overseas, where they are very popular as they depict so many typical British people and their stories, and are set in wonderful landscape with music splendidly arranged and performed. The difference between the 1977 *Songs of Praise* in which I sang in Worcester Cathedral and one today is incredible – the one black and white, with static camera-work, the presenter almost giving a sermon from the pulpit; and the other in glorious colour, the hymns accompanied by special orchestrations, wonderful outdoor shots and the congregation obviously enjoying themselves.

After my first presentation in Arundel I did Goudhurst in Kent, a very pretty village in the Garden of England. There I met a prisoner who was helping people in the village as part of his rehabilitation, and talked to the local C. of E. vicar and the Roman Catholic priest, who are working to bring the religious communities together. In Lacock in Wiltshire a young lady who had lost nearly everything when her thatched cottage burned down was helped by the villagers; the church has a woman priest; and while a potter threw a pot on a wheel I talked about the religious feeling that I get from a pot – a mystical thing; after all, the good book says that we ourselves are made from the dust of the earth. In Bath we celebrated the tenth year of BBC Radio 2's Choirgirl of the Year competition – the nine previous winners singing in the church and the tenth being announced in the programme. In the Rhondda valley in Wales we celebrated the reunion of wartime evacuees who had been sent to the area and, of course, we all sang Cwm Rhondda with great spirit. For that programme I did an interview in a deserted East End school with Lord Tonypandy, who told me how he had allocated homes for the 'little orphans' coming down to the Rhondda from London. As our voices echoed around the bare school room, you could feel the ghosts of those little children. I talked to a one-time East End evacuee while we sat in a pie-and-eel shop – ah, what memories it brought back!

My favourite *Songs of Praise* was a series of four

programmes entitled 'Hymnformation', which gave the stories behind the writing of many of our favourite hymns. The programmes started with me sitting in the pavilion of Worcester county cricket ground watching a match, with the Cathedral in the background. I explained that my time in the cathedral had led to my interest in hymns with the putting up of scores on the hymn board, and over the next four weeks we would share some wonderful stories and hear some fine singing. This is called 'the Tease', intended to hook the viewers and make them go on watching. Most of the main choral hymn singing was in Kidderminster's church of St Mary and All Saints, where the hymn-writer Richard Baxter had once served, and the Methodist Church at Epworth in Lincolnshire, the home of the Wesley family, where Methodist choirs sang Wesley hymns with great spirit.

For the presentations and interviews we went to a fascinating range of places – the summit of the Malvern Hills to talk about Elgar and *Gerontius*; the magnificent Baroque splendour of Witley Hall church in Worcestershire to hear Handel's organ and a small choir sing; St Paul's Cathedral choir school to interview Paul Way who was the chorister in the lovely BBC serial *The Choir*; Downing Street, outside the old Commonwealth Office, to introduce 'I vow to thee my country', written by an ex-civil servant who had worked there; a London school to introduce children's hymns such as 'All things bright and beautiful' (and it was lovely to see kids playing playground games that I thought had died out); the Rectory in Epworth to talk about the incredible Wesley family of preachers and hymn-writers; the 'Little Teapot' tearooms in Epworth to talk about a hymn that aimed to turn people away from drug-induced religious fervour.

We also met a number of bishops who wrote hymns; they were jolly, happy men. I asked one of them, the Bishop of Worcester, what made a good and a bad hymn. He said a good hymn was stirring, with strong ideas which got you worked up; a bad hymn was inappropriate for the occasion. He cited one that was popular at weddings when he was a young priest – 'The voice that breathed o'er Eden'; when he got to the line 'There stands the Awful Father' he didn't dare look at the bride's father. I met a publisher of modern hymns and the writer and composer of one of the most beautiful hymns I have heard, 'Knowing you Jesus', which I haven't been able to get out of my mind.

The stories behind the writing of dozens of hymns fascinated both me and the viewers, who wrote in their hundreds to say which particular hymn was their favourite. We had 'Nearer my God to thee' and the sinking of the *Titanic* described by Eva Hart, a survivor, who has since died; 'Amazing Grace', written after a storm at sea turned a sailor from a life of debauchery to one of deep religious commitment. My favourite presentation was done in one take, the story behind 'Stand up, stand up for Jesus'. The producer had me seated on a bale of hay in a farm-yard, looking comfortable with my jacket off in the hot sunshine, and she told me to relax and enjoy it and put in any bits of my own that I wanted. So I told the story about this great preacher in Philadelphia in the 1840s who preached to huge outdoor gatherings – a bit like Billy Graham in our own day (my own bit). He was going home one evening, passed through a farmyard and stopped to pat a mule that was pulling some farm machinery. His gown got caught in the machinery and his arm was torn off (I made it very dramatic). He was lying on the ground, dying from loss of blood, when his friend came and looked down at him and said, 'Have you got a message I can give to your friends back at the mission?'

'Tell them to stand up for Jesus!'

His friend later wrote the great hymn in memory of a dead friend – Stand up, stand up for Jesus.

And that should have been the end and the choir were meant to burst in with the hymn, but I just had to say something else. It came into my mind and I said, 'Wasn't it a good job that he hadn't lost his leg!' There was silence, a loud silence, and finally Diane Reid, the producer, said, 'You can't say that!'

'I'm sorry,' I said, 'I just had to say it!'

'Well, we'll cut it out,' she said, and of course they did, just lopping the naughty sentence off the end. Weeks later I agreed to her sending it up to *Auntie's Bloomers*, in which comical mistakes and outtakes are shown, so I hope I am forgiven now.

On 21st November 1995 I was asked to present some of the Gold Awards for the Duke of Edinburgh's Award scheme at St James's Palace in London. The Duke proceeds through all the rooms, meets some of the wonderful young men and women who have worked so hard through different stages of tests to obtain their gold award. In each of the magnificent rooms of the Palace a hundred youngsters are gathered on one side and their families on the other, and a well known person, such as a sportsman or TV personality, has the task of giving a short speech before the Duke appears. Then, after he leaves, the speaker shakes hands with each recipient, presents them with the award and says a few words of congratulation. Barbara came with me and it was thrilling to share this great day with such wonderful youngsters, who prove that this country can produce fine people for the future. The day had been quite a packed one, the morning being a recording of *The Great Antiques Hunt* at Epsom racecourse, which was unusually challenging because David Battie and I were given the £100 and sent into the antiques fair to buy something for the contestants to sell at the subsequent auction. This was difficult, as it wasn't a case of buying something that you wanted yourself but what would make a profit at auction. My pair won, with a pair of Moore Brothers candlesticks that I bought for them, but it was the closest result in the whole series.

As I write this autobiography I have again been asked to present the Duke of Edinburgh's Gold Awards in July. This time it is to be held at Buckingham Palace in the early afternoon and Barbara and I have been invited to the Royal Garden Party that follows. The honour of being invited to such things has meant a lot to us and when we married we couldn't have dreamed that such things were going to happen. When we did our lecture cruise on P & O's *Victoria* in August 1996 my first lecture was on 2nd August, our wedding anniversary, and I told the audience that the day was a very special one for us because it was our *eightieth* wedding anniversary. I could see the puzzled looks and hear the mumbled voices – 'He can't be as old as that!' Then I put them out of their misery by saying that it was forty years for me and forty years for her, making eighty. We celebrated that night with a special bottle of Ruby Wine – a vintage suggested by Jilly Goolden.

This year we are off on a three-week Antique Theme Cruise to the Caribbean, which I am sure is going to be exciting. Having suffered with an arthritic hip, which had been getting more painful for some time, I had a hip replacement in the Worcester Royal Infirmary this January. The hospital is historically very important: it was founded in 1770 by Dr John Wall, the founder of the Worcester Porcelain Company, and in the boardroom the British Medical Association was founded. My wife and I have great reason to be grateful to the hospital and the kindness and skill of all who work there in old and worn-out buildings, but it is the staff who make a great hospital, even if it is in a humble cowshed. My hip operation was successful, but it had its funny sides, as when I was asked to look at a nurse's china before I was wheeled down to the operating room – I think they were not sure that I would return. I wanted a new porcelain hip but one couldn't be made in time; but the odd bits of bones they took out have gone into the bone bank to help other people. When I agreed to this I thought of Tony Hancock, worried that his blood donation was going to go to a worthy person. Will the lucky person who gets mine please let me know, and we'll celebrate it! The hospital authorities asked me and Snowie to open the special open day and we had a great time. Later I have to start the charity Hip Walk along the river bank and my mate 'Dick' Barton said I should start it by shouting, 'Get fell in!'

I expect that a lot of people born in 1928 have retired by now. I am glad that I haven't, as there are so many places that I want to see, things to do and pots to collect. I would love to go to Peru and see the great Pre-Columbian cultures and ceramics that I have admired for so long. I would give my bottom set of teeth (they are still all my own) to play the Demon King in pantomime and Dolittle in *My Fair Lady*, but please don't tell Barbara as I know she won't let me. What I have done in the last few months is to become a director of a small china factory – the Brontë Porcelain Company of Malvern. A bunch of superb craftsmen and women are making the finest bone china ornaments and plaques that I have seen since the days of Doris Lindner and Harry Davis, and this has given me great joy. To work with my fellow directors – Terry Lewis, who learned his casting under Bob Bradley the master caster of Royal Worcester, and Bob Price, who knows all about the chemistry of colours and glazes from his thirty years with Ferro International – is something that I never thought would happen. They are making a candle extinguisher depicting me, which will join the other pots made in my image – a Toby jug and a teapot.

Great joys come pouring in, from the chap who stops me in the street and says, 'You've given my wife great pleasure for years,' to the joy of our children and grandchildren (Elizabeth has just passed her eleven plus with perfect marks in maths – she doesn't get that from me, nor from her father), to the joy that ceramics have given me over the years. I take a pot to bed with me each night – I say to them, 'Who wants to come to bed with me tonight?' and there will be cries of 'Me, me, me!'

When people thank me for the pleasure that I have given them, I thank them for giving me the opportunities to do that.

Index

Index

Gilbert, Alex 9
Gilbert, Rosie (née Mellish)
    (HS's aunt) 4, 6, 9
Gill, Wendy 151
Godden, Geoffrey 102–5
Going for a Song 113–16
Goolden, Jilly 179
Goring-by-Sea 183
Gotchas 156–60
Goudhurst 186
Graingers factory 101
Grappelli, Stephane 97
Great Antiques Hunt 178–80,
    190
Green, Topliss 48, 50
Greene, Eric 66–7
Gresham Life Assurance 84, 91
Grimson, Joseph 91
Guest, Douglas 81
Guildhall School of Music 51

Handley, Joseph 167
Harley, Helen 49
Harrogate 179
Hart, Eva 188
Heath, Edward 106–7
Heirlooms 164
Henshall, Helen 50–1
Hereford United football team
    99
High Wycombe 21
High Wycombe Royal
    Grammar School 21, 24–7
Hofheimer, Henry Clay 167
Holness, Bob 161, 166
Holywood Barracks 42
Hulbert, Claude 13–14
Hunt, Donald 122
Hyde, Walter 51
hymns 187–9

Inverness 153

Jamaica 154
John, King 82–3
Johnston, Angus 121
Johnston, Brian 98, 130
Johnston, David 49, 63
Johnston, James 78

Kay, Hilary 141
Kew Palace 119
Kiddell, James 106
Kidderminster 187
King's School, Worcester 86
Kirkby, Captain 62
Klepser, Priscilla and Kenneth
    167
Knowles, Eric 141, 160, 180

Lacock 186
Laine, Cleo 162
Landon, Dinsdale 163
Lang, Gordon 141
Lawe, John 79
Lewis, Christopher 137, 157
Lewis, Percy 96
Lewis, Terry 96, 193
Littlecote House 123–7
Lloyd-Foulkes, Maria 89
Longton Hall factory 105

McCormack, John 130
McShee, Sheila 77
Malvern Operatic Society 89
Mary, Queen 168
Masters, Victor 37
Maundy service 100
Mellish, Alice ('Dolly') (HS's
    aunt) 4, 5–6

Index